PRAYER IS GOOD MEDICINE

Also by Larry Dossey, M.D.

Healing Words: The Power of Prayer and the Practice of Medicine
Space, Time & Medicine
Beyond Illness
Recovering the Soul
Meaning & Medicine

PRAYER
IS GOOD MEDICINE

—✺—

HOW TO REAP

THE HEALING BENEFITS

OF PRAYER

Larry Dossey, M.D.

HarperSanFrancisco
An Imprint of HarperCollins*Publishers*

HarperCollins Web Site: http://www.harpercollins.com

HarperCollins®, ⚒ ®, and HarperSanFrancisco™ are trademarks of HarperCollins Publishers Inc.

First HarperCollins Paperback Edition Published in 1997

Library of Congress Cataloging-in-Publication Data
Dossey, Larry
Prayer is good medicine : how to reap the healing benefits of prayer / Larry Dossey. — 1st ed.
Includes bibliographical references.
ISBN 0–06–251423–7 (cloth)
ISBN 0–06–251424–5 (pbk.)
1. Healing—Religious aspects.   2. Prayer.   I. Title.
BL65.M4D674   1996
291.4'3 — dc20

96–12273

02 03 ❖ HAD 15 14 13

To my colleagues in health care
who have had the courage to carry prayer
into the hospital, clinic, and laboratory.

CONTENTS

Contents

CONTENTS

ACKNOWLEDGMENTS

I offer a prayer of thanksgiving for the many people who have provided encouragement to me in addressing the issue of prayer in medicine.

To Garry and Bet: We didn't know we were being influenced so deeply by all those prayers while growing up at Prairie Point, did we? Or was it Prayer-y Point?

To my mother and father, who kept my brother and me—two-pound, premature twins—alive with prayers and a warm fireplace on a dreary Texas prairie.

And to Barbara, my wife, who remains the answer to my prayer.

—Larry Dossey, M.D.
    Santa Fe, New Mexico

AUTHOR'S NOTE

Many terms are used throughout this book to refer to a Supreme Being. In most cases I have chosen as neutral a term as possible, such as *the Absolute*.

I tend to agree with those wise teachers who say that all the names of God are misleading. As all the major esoteric wisdom traditions tell us, the Absolute "cannot be spoken or thought." There are simply no reliable pictures of the Almighty. As the Sufi aphorism soberly states, "No man has seen God and lived."

In the fourteenth century, an anonymous English monk believed to be the author of *The Cloud of Unknowing*, an exalted religious tract that deeply influenced the religious life of the time, added his lament to the futility of addressing and even thinking about the Universal. "But now you will ask me," said he, " 'How am I to think of God himself, and what is he?' and I cannot answer you except to say 'I do not know!' For with this question you have brought me into the . . . cloud of unknowing. . . . Of God himself can no man think."

As the great thirteenth-century German mystic Meister Eckhart observed, "Whoever perceives something in God and attaches thereby some name to him, that is not God. God is . . . ineffable." And, "It is God's nature to be without a nature."

At this moment in history, in which we're experiencing a much-needed awakening of values that for centuries have been associated with women, perhaps it is important to point out that the problem of naming the Absolute is not resolved merely by replacing all the masculine names and pronouns with feminine ones. *God* and *Goddess*, *he* and *she*, founder equally. The Absolute is radically beyond any description whatsoever, including gender.

With these limitations in mind, the reader may insert, in every instance that follows, his or her preferred name for the Absolute—whether *Goddess, God, Allah, Krishna, Brahman, the Tao, the Universal Mind, the Almighty, Alpha and Omega, the One* . . .

PRAYER IS GOOD MEDICINE

If Jesus, Muhammad, and Buddha had had penicillin, they probably would have used it—along with prayer.

I believe that prayer and standard medical approaches can be used together. So, although this book deals with why prayer is good medicine, I am not suggesting that it is the *only* medicine or that it must be relied on *instead of* other medicines.

Prayer is not "better" than modern medicine. Prayer, medications, and surgery—they are all a blessing, a grace, a gift. Why not use all of them, with reverence and gratitude?

INTRODUCTION

Prayer is back.

After sitting on the sidelines for most of this century, prayer is moving toward center stage in modern medicine. Doctors are taking prayer not just into their offices, clinics, and hospitals, but into experimental laboratories as well. Medical journals are more willing than ever to publish studies on the healing effects of prayer and faith. Cover stories on prayer have appeared in several national news magazines, and talks shows buzz with accounts of healing and prayer. Even the conservative *Wall Street*

Journal recently devoted a major article in its "Market-place" section to the scientific studies of prayer that are currently in progress.

Most of you would probably say, It's about time. Recent surveys show that 75 percent of patients believe their physicians should address spiritual issues as part of medical care, and 50 percent want their doctor to pray not just for them but with them. We doctors appear to be listening. You may be surprised to know that the majority of us actually pray for our patients. In December 1995 a conference entitled "Spirituality and Healing in Medicine" was held at Harvard Medical School in Boston, one of our best medical institutions. As of this writing, about one-third of the medical schools in the United States have developed courses in alternative/complementary medicine, many of which emphasize spiritual issues in health care, including prayer. Five medical schools have developed programs explicitly dedicated to exploring the relationship between faith and health.

Are we falling into fantasy? Hardly. "Statistically, God is good for you," says David B. Larson, M.D., of the National Institute for Healthcare Research in Rockville, Maryland, which studies the relationship between spirituality and health. Larson, a former senior researcher at the National Institute of Mental Health, says, "I was told by my [medical school] professors that religion is harmful. Then I looked at the research, and religion is actually highly beneficial. If you go to church or pray regularly, it's very beneficial in terms of preventing illness, mental and physical, and you cope with illness much more effectively. If you look at the research, in area after area, it's 80 percent beneficial. I was shocked."

So was I. I stumbled blindly into the research on prayer during the 1980s, when someone sent me a scientific paper in which prayer was tested in a modern hospital in a large group of heart patients. It had never occurred to me that anyone would actually test prayer like a new medication—praying for half the patients and not for the other half, who were the "controls," and measuring the results. This study strongly suggested a therapeutic effect of distant, intercessory prayer.

After I recovered from my surprise, I asked myself, If prayer works, shouldn't I be praying for my patients? I was skeptical of prayer at the time, and a single study was not convincing. Needing further proof, I embarked on my own research and discovered, to my further amazement, that there are more than 130 scientific studies in the general area of "healing," many of which employ prayer. Over half of these experiments strongly indicate that prayer works. I soon came to regard this evidence as one of the best-kept secrets in modern medicine, and I began actively to pray for my patients.

My explorations of prayer and healing resulted in the 1993 publication of my book *Healing Words: The Power of Prayer and the Practice of Medicine.* To my great pleasure, the strong reception to the book afforded me the opportunity to discuss prayer with a variety of audiences—medical schools and hospitals, physician and nurse organizations, lay groups and churches, the National Institutes of Health, a Presidential Task Force on Health Care Reform, a section of the British Parliament, and even the Pentagon.

Certain questions surfaced again and again in these discussions. I know they are on your mind, too, because you sent me hundreds of letters describing your experiences and beliefs about prayer. I discovered that most of you are interested in four general areas—the scientific evidence for prayer, the controversies associated with the prayer experiments, what prayer is, and how to pray. This book is organized around these four categories. The various sections stand on their own and can be read in any order. Be your own guide.

I have written this book as a heart-to-heart talk, not as an academic or scholarly treatise. If you want to look deeper at the scientific issues surrounding prayer, you may consult *Healing Words*, where you can find descriptions and citations of the experiments themselves.

As you read this book, I hope you will resist the temptation to take an either-or stance toward prayer and modern medicine. As a physician, I have employed medications and surgical procedures because I know they work. But prayer works, too. The way I see it, we do not have to make absolute choices between prayer and high-tech medicine. If you have appendicitis, I believe you should have an appendectomy, because it is the most effective treatment humankind has ever devised for this particular problem. But why not employ prayer in addition to surgery? Prayerlike thoughts, offered from a distance, have been demonstrated to increase the healing rate of surgical wounds, and religious faith is associated with faster recovery from surgery. We ought to follow a common sense approach when we're sick: Use what works. In most medical situations there will be a place for *both* prayer and modern medicine.

Although science tells us *that* prayer works, it cannot tell us *how* it works. Science is limited in studying prayer.

Therefore, science can never swallow up prayer, as some people fear. The sacred mysteries will remain.

I have written this book while under the influence— the influence of the prayers of thousands of people who have prayed for me and for my work. From my heart, I am grateful. Will you keep me under the influence?

—Larry Dossey, M.D.

PART ONE

—⫘—

THE EVIDENCE

TESTING PRAYER IS AN ACT OF WORSHIP

What if your physician told you the next time you're sick, "Take a handful of drugs. Pay no mind to whether they're mixed or matched, and don't bother to count them. Just take a lot, as often as possible, because drugs heal." Even if you believe in drug therapy, you'd consider this advice irresponsible and dangerous. There are many kinds of drugs—some helpful, some worthless, some harmful. Some drugs work singly; others work only in combination; some are toxic or fatal if combined with other medications. Only by careful testing can these effects be sorted out and the drugs used safely and effectively.

The same could be said of prayer. There are different kinds of prayer, and evidence suggests that prayer, like drugs, can have effects that can be positive, neutral, or negative. Based on evidence, it might even be wise to attach a warning to prayer: "Could be hazardous to your health."

One of the best ways to understand the nuances of prayer and to learn how best to use it is to examine it carefully in scientific experiments. Everyone should be interested in this evidence, it seems to me, even those who already believe in prayer.

Some people believe that science is the enemy of faith and that prayer should not be tested scientifically. But scientists also require faith. In fact, I have often thought that many scientists have more faith than some religious folk. For example, they have faith in the regularity and patterns of the universe; faith that knowledge is possible; faith that nature will reveal *itself* if we prepare *ourselves* and our experiments properly. Without faith, science would not be possible. Faith is a foundation of science, as it is of prayer.

When we test prayer, we are not necessarily storming heaven's gates. It is possible for scientific studies of prayer to be totally devoid of arrogance and hubris. They can be sacred, reverent exercises in which we invite, not compel, the Almighty to manifest. Testing prayer can actually be a form of worship, a ritual through which we express our gratitude for this remarkable phenomenon.

A friend of mine who is a scientist performs experiments on prayer. He embodies the reverential approach I am advocating. "For me," he once said, "conducting an experiment to see if prayer works is like giving an elegant dinner party. I prepare the most inviting meal I can imagine, I set the table as beautifully as possible, then I open the front doors of my house to see if anybody will come to the table. If not, the dinner wasn't enticing enough. An experiment in prayer is similar. If I arrange the conditions of the experiment invitingly enough, the Divine may 'show up' and I'll get positive results. If not, I've got more work to do next time."

Teilhard de Chardin, the Jesuit priest and scholar, once said something similar: "Research is the highest form of adoration."

EXPERIMENTS IN PRAYER CAN HELP HEAL
THE RELIGION/SCIENCE SPLIT

The vast majority of us pray, and we believe our prayers are answered. We aren't holding our breath in anticipation of the results of the next double-blind laboratory study on prayer. We feel that we already have evidence for prayer in our lives, and our lives are the most important laboratories of all.

Still, we cannot escape the influence of science in our lives. The scientific approach has infiltrated every aspect of our existence. Before taking a stand on a controversial issue—global warming, for instance, or alternative treatments for cancer—we find ourselves asking, "What does science say?"

Prayer, like almost everything else, is being scrutinized by science. Some scientists and physicians have begun to acknowledge that petitionary prayer, in which one prays for oneself, has positive, healthful effects, but many of them add that this is due *only* to psychological factors such as positive thinking, expectation, and self-suggestion. Some of these same scientists tend to believe that inter-cessory or distant prayer cannot possibly be effective; the mind cannot reach out, whether of its own accord or through a Supreme Being, to make things happen at a distance. If we believe in distant prayer, they say, we are fooling ourselves. But when put to the test in actual experiments in hospitals, clinics, and laboratories, distant prayer *does* have an effect—in humans and nonhumans, even when the recipient of the prayer is unaware the prayer is being offered.

These developments are incalculably important in healing the painful split in modern life between religion and science. We don't have to compartmentalize our lives, putting our intellect in one corner and our spirituality in another. The scientific evidence behind prayer can help heal these painful divisions in the modern psyche. That is why many people, believers included, often joyfully welcome the experimental evidence for prayer. They find that their faith is actually strengthened, not diminished, by science's attention to prayer.

Honoring this evidence does not mean we are allowing science to hold prayer hostage. Prayer doesn't need science's stamp of approval. But if the old enemies can shake hands, we should allow them to do so, for we shall all benefit spiritually from the truce.

THE IMPACT OF PRAYER EXPERIMENTS
ON RELIGIOUS BELIEFS

It is really no longer a question of *whether* experiments prove that prayer works; *they have already done so.* The new questions are: What is the fallout? What will be the impact of scientific experiments on religious faith and organized religion?

Many individuals and organizations have been involved in examining prayer through the aid of scientific studies. One such organization is Spindrift, which over the course of two decades developed a number of experimental tests showing the positive effects of prayer on nonhuman subjects. Before beginning their actual experiments in 1975, the researchers at Spindrift devoted five years to exploring the ethical concerns that would be raised by their scientific work. "Were the tests a form of temptation or were they a loving gift to a modern world from a good God?" asks Spindrift's former vice president, Deborah Rose. Is it heresy to "test God" in the laboratory? Would the experimental approach destroy faith? No other organization has so honestly confronted these questions.

In 1994 the organization received a letter from a woman in Topeka, Kansas, who was concerned that the Spindrift tests would result in the secularization of religion. She was worried about religion falling into the hands of laboratory scientists, and she did not want to see the beauty of her religious teachings replaced with cold, hard data.

In response to concerns such as this woman's, Rose acknowledges that people frequently believe Spindrift's experiments are attempts to prove, tempt, or limit God with test tubes. But the tests are not set up that way, she adds. "We are not setting a trap to catch God in, we are opening a window to watch God work."

The researchers at Spindrift do not worry that their prayer experiments will disempower religion. They are more concerned about the *opposite* effect. "[We feel our] tests will give power back to religion. That in itself is terribly dangerous. The church has not used power wisely."

For the researchers at Spindrift, these are risks worth taking. "If we want to bring the ability to heal spiritually back into the world," Rose states, "we must make a place for it. It is just like keeping a rare bird from becoming extinct. You must do more than protect the bird. You must protect and expand its habitat. We must make a place in the world for spiritual healing. The data from the Spindrift tests is a way of staking a claim to territory."

The prayer experiments do not threaten prayer, in Rose's view. "Expressing theology in 'cold hard data' will [not] replace scripture or stained glass windows or hymns or personal testimonies or all the beautiful expressions of religion in our society. It will make them flourish because it will carve out a bigger habitat in which such things can grow. There will be new expressions, too, new computerized scientific expressions, of theology. Some will find this offensive. Others . . . will find it beautiful and meaningful. Why not have both? Not everyone sees data as cold or impersonal. In my religion," Rose states, "one of the names for God is Principle. . . . At the heart of [the experimental] data I see glimpses of the Principle, or God. . . ."

Rose continues, "Proof brings [old] theological questions to light. We may discover that we were wrong about many things. Who decided in the past what was holy and who was holy, what was sinful and who was sinful? It was sometimes a political matter. . . . I look forward to tools such as the Spindrift tests which will help make religion less manipulative, less secular, and more pure."

Rose is also concerned that people may use the tests to

promote a single type of religion. "By scientifically proving religion we could lose the freedom of religion, and we could lose all the beauty and individuality of differing religious traditions. . . . This sad scene does not have to come to pass. The tests have shown that people from many religious traditions do equally well on these tests."

Another danger of the experiments is that people may use them to devise ways of harming others. Says Rose, "This research will make the dark side of mental power more obvious and accessible to people. . . . It is possible to make someone sick through mental means, and even to kill them. . . . Once the Spindrift tests or tests like them become common knowledge through replication, the subject of the dark side of thought is bound to come up. Those with the proclivity will be able to learn more easily the destructive use of mental power."

In spite of the potential pitfalls, researchers at Spindrift, after two decades of experimenting with prayer, conclude that the benefits of testing far outweigh the problems. "Anything," Rose observes, "which brings truth to the surface, and helps us to understand more about the nature of the universe in which we live, is an inevitable blessing, however high the price. Ignorance is the biggest danger."

Following the publication of my book *Healing Words: The Power of Prayer and the Practice of Medicine,* I discovered that many of Rose's predictions were true. Fundamentalist groups from around the country reacted with outrage, condemning the scientific evidence as "occult" and "New Age" without stopping to consider whether or not the studies were valid. The primary reason they were offended seems to be that the prayer experiments show, as Rose states, that "people from many religious traditions do equally well on these tests." In other words, the experiments make clear that no specific religion has a monopoly on prayer. This is contrary to the belief of many fundamentalists that the Almighty is attuned mainly or exclusively to them; that those who are not "saved" can't really pray effectively; and that the only genuine prayer people outside their faith can offer is for mercy and forgiveness. To anyone holding such beliefs, the prayer experiments represent a colossal conflict between science and faith. When these two worlds collide, it is usually science that gets tossed out and dogma that is retained.

I am convinced that the experiments in prayer do not oppose genuine spirituality; they are a threat only to narrowness and exclusivity, which are the backbone of religious intolerance. It is not the Absolute who is threatened by the scientific evidence favoring prayer, only our own arrogance and pride and the special status that some religions have claimed for themselves. Prayer experiments level the praying field. They show that prayer is a universal phenomenon belonging to every faith and creed, and these studies, therefore, affirm tolerance.

THE SCIENTIFIC UNDERSTANDING
OF PRAYER IS LIMITED

I have found that most people within the major religions in our country are extremely tolerant toward the prayer experiments. They are eager for a rapprochement between science and religion in which the intellectual and spiritual vectors in the human psyche might come together in harmony. Some of them see prayer experimentation as an advance for religion itself. They agree with Emerson that "the religion that is afraid of science dishonors God and commits suicide." And they agree with anthropologist Margaret Mead, who said, "We need a religious system with science at its very core, in which the traditional opposition between science and religion . . . can again be resolved, but in terms of the future instead of the past."

Perhaps those who fear that science will engulf religion do not understand the limits of science. When we investigate prayer scientifically we can show only *that* it works, not *how* or *why* it works. This means there is a threshold beyond which science cannot pass. These limits are illustrated in the following interchange between a science professor and the student-candidate he was examining:

> *Examiner*: What is electricity?
> *Candidate*: Oh, Sir, I'm sure I have learn't what it is—I'm sure I did know—but I've forgotten.
> *Examiner*: How very unfortunate. Only two persons have ever known what electricity is, the Author of Nature and yourself. Now one of them has forgotten.

Science raises more questions about prayer than it answers. Science cannot measure the unmeasurable. This leaves many facets of prayer largely untouched, and it creates an opening for the various religions to connect the dots any way they wish.

To be sure, some scientists don't agree. They believe, through a curious twist of logic, that science has disproved the Almighty, even though the Absolute is beyond measurement and therefore beyond science. But we should not be pushed around by this prejudice. We might look instead to a view that has been held by scientists of the highest caliber, in which *both* the power and the limitations of science are acknowledged. A typical expression of this perspective is the following comment by Nobel physicist Erwin Schrödinger. Schrödinger's observations might serve as a consolation to those who fear mixing science and prayer:

> We shall not expect the natural sciences to give us direct insight into the nature of the spirit; we shall not *hope* to penetrate it, however much we learn about the physics and chemistry of the bodily processes with which we find perception and thought objectively linked; and we shall not *fear* that even the most exact knowledge of the mechanism of these processes and the laws by which they operate—a knowledge the subject of which is and will always remain in the spirit—can lay fetters upon the spirit itself, that is, can compel us to regard it as unfree, "mechanically determined," on the ground that it is linked with a physiological process that is mechanically determined and subject to laws of nature.

Max Planck, whose discoveries set the stage for the quantum-relativistic revolution in physics, saw that science and religion were naturally intertwined. He said,

There can never be any real opposition between religion and science; for one is the complement of the other. Every serious and reflective person realizes, I think, that the religious element in nature must be recognized and cultivated if all the powers of the human soul are to act together in perfect balance and harmony. And indeed it was not by any accident that the greatest thinkers of all ages were also deeply religious souls, even though they made no public show of their religious feeling. . . . Every advance in knowledge brings us face to face with the mystery of our own being.

The list of great physicists who took similar views is very long. It includes giants such as Einstein, Bohr, Heisenberg, Eddington, Jeans, and others. Their views have been brought together in a stunning book, *Quantum Questions: The Mystical Writings of the World's Great Physicists*, by transpersonal psychologist Ken Wilber.

It is often said that science has "disproved God," but this is an impossibility, as these great scientists knew. Science deals only with what can be measured by its various detection devices—and scientists do not have a God meter. Some things are beyond science. Everything that counts cannot be counted.

Those who wish to shield prayer from science and to toss the prayer experiments out the window ought to examine their motives. The first question that should be asked—and this is almost never done—is, What do the studies actually show, and are they valid? If we actually appraise the data and decide it is true, we might then ask further questions. Why are we tempted to discard experimental fact? Are we trying to "protect prayer," as if the Absolute needs our help? Which of our private religious beliefs are being threatened? Should we rethink some of them?

One of the most courageous examples of bringing religion and science to bear on one another comes from His Holiness the Dalai Lama. Unlike many religious leaders, the Dalai Lama adores science and delights in interchanges with scientists. He was once asked how Buddhism would respond if Buddhist doctrine were to collide with solid scientific facts. If this happened, he replied, the Buddha's own words must be rejected. But, he added with a twinkle in his eye, he was not worried, for through the ages Buddhism has always found plenty of room to maneuver.

Those who fear experiments in prayer might relax. Prayer and the Almighty cannot be harmed by science. Only our prejudices are in danger.

PRAYER IS NOT JUST A PLACEBO

Many people believe prayer has no power of its own. People get better following prayer, they maintain, only because people *expect* that prayer will work. We call this the "placebo effect."

The word *placebo* comes from Latin and means "I shall please." A placebo is a harmless, inert substance—a sugar pill or water injection—given to patients to please or humor them.

Placebo effects are results that can be attributed to belief, expectation, suggestion, or "positive thinking." In other words, if your doctor prescribes a placebo pill for you and you feel better after taking it, this wasn't due to the pill but to your thoughts, emotions, beliefs, and so on.

In the case of prayer, there is no doubt that the beliefs of an individual play a role: In both petitionary prayer, where one prays for oneself; and in intercessory or distant prayer, *when the recipient of the prayer knows she or he is being prayed for,* the very fact that the individual realizes the prayer may work can bring about positive effects. But this does not mean the results of prayer in these two instances are due *only* to placebo effects.

There have been countless instances in which distant or intercessory prayer succeeds *without the knowledge* of the recipient. When prayer works in these cases, it cannot possibly be due totally to placebo effects.

We should be less critical of placebo effects, as when we say something is "just" a placebo. Placebo effects are like a higher gear in an automobile, capable of boosting the performance of any therapy. We should cease referring to these effects as a nuisance, as doctors often do; placebo effects do not just get in the way of "real" medicine. We should be grateful that the powers of expectation, suggestion, and positive thinking can add to the power of prayer.

Placebo effects are a gift. Why refuse them?

PRAYER IS NOT REQUIRED TO GO ANYWHERE

Several decades ago a rollicking gospel song called "The Royal Telephone" was popular in the South. God's lines are always open, the tune proclaimed, and we can ring him up anytime. Today, images of prayer that employ clumsy black telephones and plug-in switchboards seem whimsical and outmoded and are fast being replaced by more up-to-date pictures. Currently, "God as communication satellite" is particularly trendy. We beam our prayers upward—up, up, always up—and if he approves, he relays the request to the object in need. There are other popular images. I recently came across a cartoon in which a young boy is holding a sheet of paper and is saying to his mom, "I wrote down a prayer. Does God have a fax machine?"

In an old Buddhist tale, several monks are mourning their elderly master, who had died earlier that day. A question arises: "Where has the soul of the master gone?" The debate rages for hours with no consensus. The young monk picked by the departed master to succeed him becomes exasperated with the discussion and finally asks, "Why is it necessary for his soul to go anywhere?"

Why do we suppose it is necessary for prayer to go any-where? Is prayer a thing? Does it need to travel?

Our images of prayer suggest that it is some sort of physical message—a letter, for example—that must travel to a specific destination. Or prayers are like phone calls and television signals that are transmitted through fiber-optic cables or bounced off orbiting satellites and relay stations. To say that prayers need to be sent "to" God im-plies God is a being who is localized in some distant place.

Findings from scientific studies of prayer do not bear out this picture of prayer as a physical message sent to a God who resides at a distance. In a study by cardiolo-gist Randolph Byrd involving 393 patients in the coro-nary care unit of San Francisco General Hospital, prayer groups in various parts of the United States were asked to pray for sick individuals assigned to a "treatment" group; no one prayed for those in the control group. Except for prayer, all the patients received the same high-tech ther-apy. This was a double-blind study: No patients, no physi-cians, and no nurses knew who was and was not being prayed for. Byrd found that the prayed-for patients did significantly better on several outcome measures. Dis-tance was *not* found to be a factor in how well the prayer worked. Prayers from the other side of the country appeared to be as effective as prayers from groups close to the hospital.

Other studies have compared the ability of people to influence the growth rates of organisms at close range (1.5 yards) and at a distance (15 miles). Again, distance was not a factor; near or far, the strength of the influence was the same.

The scores of experiments dealing with spiritual healing have never detected any type of energy passing between the healer and the healee. This implies that nothing *physical* is sent between the praying individual and the object of the prayer. In addition, these studies consistently show that prayer is as effective at great distances as at close range. If some sort of physical energy were being sent, prayer would be more powerful at short ranges than long, because physical energy weakens with distance. Nor can the effects of prayer be shielded or blocked, which would not be the case if some type of energy were being sent from the healer to the healee. The experiments in prayer-based healing give a consistent picture: Prayer is not some conventional form of energy that is "sent" or "received."

To someone wedded to the idea that prayer equals energy, this sounds as if prayer doesn't work—no energy, no effect. But prayer *does* work. It is our images of prayer that don't. When we acquire the courage to accept the Absolute *as* Absolute, we won't require mundane images of prayer. We will realize that prayer, like the soul of the departed master, is not required to go anywhere.

Although scientists cannot currently explain how prayer works at a distance, there are developments in certain areas that may one day shed light on its operation.

In quantum physics, which concerns itself with the smallest dimensions of the physical world, several experiments in the past two decades have revealed the existence of what are termed *nonlocal* events. Briefly: If two subatomic particles that have been in contact are separated, a change in one is correlated with a change in the other, instantly and to the same degree, no matter how far apart they may be. These distant events are said to be *nonlocal*.

Nonlocal events have three common characteristics. They are said to be *unmediated* (the distant changes do not depend on the transmission of energy or on any sort of energetic signal); they are *unmitigated* (the strength of the changes does not become weaker with increasing distance); and they are *immediate* (the distant changes take place simultaneously).

The most vexing question of all is, How could one of the distant particles be instantly aware of the change in its faraway partner? How could the two stay in instant synchrony? If the particles change simultaneously no matter how far apart they are, this suggests that they are not really separate but are in some sense a single particle or of "one mind." Mind-boggling? Yes, even for the physicists involved.

Nobel physicist Brian Josephson of Cambridge University's Cavendish Laboratory suggests that these nonlocal *quantum* phenomena may underlie many *human* events taking place at a distance—for example, types of extrasensory perception such as clairvoyance and telepathy.

Might distant, intercessory prayer also be explained by underlying quantum phenomena? No specific form of energy has ever been identified in its "transmission." And since it appears as effective at global distances as at the bedside, distance is apparently not a limiting factor. Intercessory prayer, therefore, bears strong resemblance to the nonlocal events studied by physicists.

The quantum-based "explanations" for intercessory prayer, however, have one major limitation. To say that distant prayer may be based on nonlocal quantum connections is merely to replace one mystery with another. Physicists don't actually know *how* nonlocal quantum events happen; they know only *that* they do. This brings to mind an old saying: "Physicists never really understand a new theory, they just get used to it."

Today, the term *quantum* is used to describe everything imaginable; no doubt we shall soon hear about "quantum prayer." This reflects a certain physics envy within our culture. Philosopher Stephen E. Braude of the University of Maryland calls this the "small is beautiful" way of thinking—the belief that if something can be linked to the invisible subatomic domain it is somehow more respectable. But at the quantum level the mystery does not fade, it deepens. Quantum offers the illusion of understanding. Quantum is not a "how."

Other hypotheses for prayer exist. Some researchers in parapsychology have suggested that distant prayer is "just" an example of psychokinesis, or mind over matter. But how does that work? Others have suggested that the exchange of *information*, not energy, is involved in the action of intercessory prayer at great distances. Perhaps.

But again this seems to be replacing one unknown with another.

We probably won't know how distant prayer works until we understand how consciousness works, because love, empathy, and deep caring appear to catalyze or set the stage for prayer's effects. The search for an explanation for distant prayer is really a quest for understanding the ways of the mind.

In the light of our current ignorance in science about how distant prayer works, those who wish to believe "God does it" should hold their ground. This explanation appears to be as good as any, and better than most.

PART TWO

THE CONTROVERSY

EVALUATING THE CRITICISM
THAT "PRAYER KILLS"

Skeptics never tire of putting the very worst face on prayer. One of their most common criticisms is that proponents of prayer seduce people away from using "real" therapies such as drugs and surgical procedures. Those who advocate prayer are, therefore, causing people to die. It's the argument that prayer is homicide.

Does prayer kill? Compared to what? Any answer we give must take into account the record of orthodox medicine. Each year, almost two million individuals who enter hospitals in this country acquire infections they did not have when they went there. Of these, eighty thousand die. This is the equivalent of a large passenger plane crashing every day, more fatalities than in either the Korean or Vietnam War, more than four times the number killed in auto accidents every year, and more than half as many as have died in the United States from AIDS. In many hospitals, over a third of all the admissions to critical care units are due to iatrogenic causes, which are problems caused by physicians and the drug-and-surgical treatments we employ. In any other sphere of modern life this situation would rank as a national scandal. These statistics do not emerge from an orgy of physician bashing or a criticism of "the system"; they are simply data. The point is: If one were to keep score between prayer and modern medicine, tabulating the deaths directly attributable to each, there would be no need for extra innings, overtime, or tiebreakers. Modern medicine would win the death derby every time by a landslide.

The *Physicians' Desk Reference*—the venerable *PDR*—is the medical profession's guide to prescription drugs, and it has been published annually for a half-century. The forty-ninth edition, for the year 1995, runs to nearly three thousand pages and several pounds. A considerable percentage of this tonnage is devoted to "Warnings," "Contraindications," "Precautions," and "Adverse Reactions" for each drug. The side effects may be trivial—a skin rash or nausea—or fatal. Someday, prayer may wind up in a kind of *PDR* that describes its hazards. If it does, it is inconceivable that it will have as many side effects ascribed to it as the therapies we currently use.

For years critics have leveled identical charges against prayer and alternative cancer therapies and have tended to lump these two approaches together as fraudulent. They claim that both kill because they lure people away from the tried-and-true methods of chemotherapy, surgery, and irradiation. Alternative therapists, it is said, prey on uneducated, poor, underprivileged, naive, desperate, and irrational people. The facts say otherwise. Surveys have repeatedly shown that people who opt for alternative therapies are generally *more* educated and well-off, not less. And when people choose alternative therapies they generally do *not* abandon orthodox measures but use them in conjunction with alternatives. Neither do most people believe an either-or choice must be made between prayer and conventional medicine; when seriously ill, they generally use both.

The facts show that Americans do not suddenly take up prayer when they become sick. Most of them are already praying when illness occurs. Surveys consistently show that most of us—over 90 percent of women and over 80 percent of men—pray regularly, even when we are well. People, therefore, do not turn suddenly to prayer, out of the blue, as a substitute for conventional medicine; the vast majority have been praying all along.

Does prayer kill? Let's see how this question is applied to a drug such as penicillin. Even when highly allergic people die after using it, physicians don't say that "penicillin killed" but rather that the patient had a "bad reaction" to the substance. The medication is excused; it is the body that was at fault. If we applied the same reasoning we would never say that prayer killed anyone. If someone expired after relying totally on prayer, it is because his or her body reacted badly to it. My silliness is intentional. I wish only to point out that we should apply critical symmetry and not a double standard to all therapies—drugs, surgery, prayer, and anything else.

CELEBRATING THE DIVERSITY OF PRAYER

I shall never forget an experience I had on a radio talk show after the publication of *Healing Words: The Power of Prayer and the Practice of Medicine*. The host of the program was a deeply spiritual woman who wanted to focus on the universality of prayer. We discussed the lab studies showing that the prayers of a great variety of religions are answered, and we talked about the ecumenical implications of these findings. Then she opened the phone lines, and they were jammed in no time. Callers were furious. How dare we suggest that the prayers of non-Christians are answered! There must be something wrong with the experiments! If prayers of nonbelievers appear to be answered, the prayer isn't "real" but is Satan working in disguise. The host wilted; never had her program evoked such a venomous response.

I was reminded of a telling incident that took place when one particular research team was doing experiments in prayer. Unknown to them at the time, a nearby religious group was actually praying vigorously that the experiments would fail. There was irony in their efforts. If they really believed that the activities of the experimenters were blasphemous and ineffective, why did they find it necessary to sabotage them? It was as if these prayer vigilantes knew that different kinds of prayers *are* answered, and they didn't want this fact demonstrated scientifically.

Can agnostics pray? This raises the question of whether prayer requires the belief in a personal god. Buddhists, who pray avidly, belong to a nontheistic religion. They do not address their prayers to a personal god but to the Universe. Buddhism reminds us that one need not hold an image of a personal god in order to pray.

Michael, a friend of mine, is an agnostic who prays "just in case" someone is listening. Michael tells me he wants to cover all his bases. He addresses his prayers "To Whom It May Concern." He is among the thousands of agnostics in our society who pray, a fact that has been confirmed by surveys that assess the religious habits of Americans.

Many agnostics, like Michael, are deeply spiritual. They often have a sense of universal order, beauty, and majesty that simply does not coalesce into the image of a personal god. When they pray they sometimes feel at one with "all there is," an experience that may reach tremendous depths. This conviction of an underlying unity lies at the heart of the mystical traditions of all the major religions. Surely we do not wish to insist that these mystically inclined individuals are not praying simply because their beliefs about the nature of the Ultimate may not conform to our own.

I regard "mystical agnostics" like Michael as sincere seekers of truth who have penetrated to deep levels of understanding without the religious images that most people find consoling. Their spiritual aesthetic is spartan and spare compared with the norm, and their courage is often very great. Agnostics frequently pray, sometimes devoutly. They can teach us a lot about religious tolerance, if we listen.

Most of us know in our hearts that it is deeply wrong to condemn other human beings because of how they pray. We are shamed by religious wars in which innocent men, women, and children are tortured and slain in the name of the one true way. Why is it so difficult to honor this inner voice? Why do we so easily become intolerant of The People Not Like Us?

Millions of people around the world speak English but with marvelously different accents. Can we not also regard prayer, with its many inflections, as a common, universal tongue? Can we not delight in our differences and celebrate our diversity?

It is a mistake to criticize religion as the only reservoir for fundamentalism in our society. Fundamentalist beliefs can be found in any area, including science. There are always scientists who believe they know—in advance—how the universe should behave, no experiments needed. Individuals of this persuasion are often willing to condemn the evidence for prayer without a fair hearing or even any hearing. This has resulted in an extraordinary phenomenon, one I never expected to see: religious zealots and dogmatic scientists on the same side of the fence, allies in a common cause.

Perhaps there is a way for religious fundamentalists in our culture to save face and honor the scientific evidence for prayer at the same time. The *love* and *compassion* that one brings to prayer are extremely important. The scientific studies indicate that if these are not present, prayers have little or no effect. Since Christians believe that "God is love," any prayer that is prayed in love will have God present in it. Christians can then retain the belief that God is always present in prayer, even in the prayers of agnostics or nontheists such as Buddhists.

Science shows, then, that prayer does not belong exclusively to any particular religion but to a unity of all religions, classes, and creeds. Science universalizes and democratizes prayer. It is a statement for religious tolerance. I personally believe this is one of the greatest gifts of prayer research.

PRAYER AND FALSE HOPE

Many people believe it is misleading to say that prayer heals, since we all die in the end. They would argue that prayer is just false hope.

False hope is a controversial concept. Some people believe that hope can never be false. There is always the possibility that things may turn out better than predicted and that if we actually believe in a good outcome we may tilt the chances in our favor. Others, including many physicians, disagree. They would say that suggesting to someone with metastatic pancreatic cancer that prayer might result in a cure is unethical. It is misleading and cruel to suggest a positive outcome when statistics suggest that it is extremely unlikely.

But hope is always present in any medical situation. When giving an anticancer drug in a "hopeless" case or when performing an operation against great odds, the doctor is hoping for a positive result. If physicians were not hopeful, they would never act. Why should it be okay for doctors to invoke hope in desperate situations but wrong for patients to do so?

It is easy for physicians to get trapped in this web. It's okay to hope that surgery will work, even if the outlook is grim, but it's not okay to hope for a positive effect from prayer. Trust in prayer becomes "false hope," while trust in drugs and surgery remains "true hope." This game is not about hope but about belief, because the physician is really saying that he or she believes in drugs and surgery and not in prayer.

But what are these beliefs based on? I have discovered that most physicians who rail against false hope and prayer are generally poorly informed about the scientific evidence that prayer works. They believe, contrary to the data, that belief in prayer is only a matter of faith. It is not surprising, therefore, that prayer is widely disparaged in modern medicine as representing false hope.

In any given situation, why can't we place our faith and hope in *both* methods? We don't make drugs and surgery antithetical to each other, or surgery and irradiation. Why pit any method against prayer? Relying on orthodox methods *and* prayer covers more bases than using either one alone. As one patient succinctly wrote to me, "Choosing a cancer treatment program for me was a no-brainer. Chemotherapy works. Prayer works. They don't interfere with each other. I opted for both."

Some physicians are concerned that prayer creates so much false hope that it entices people to abandon valuable drugs and surgery. No doubt one can find sporadic cases where someone tries to wing it with prayer alone and dies as a result, but the extent of this problem is probably grossly exaggerated. We ought to balance these cases with those in which prayer is associated with healing or in which it acts synergistically with orthodox methods. Unfortunately, this is seldom done by those who have disdain for prayer. We ought also to acknowledge those cases in which individuals die when hope is withdrawn or is sabotaged by medical folk. These cases are numerous. They show that hope can sustain life and that its absence can kill.

Many critics believe prayer creates false hope because it does not work 100 percent of the time. I find this an extremely odd point of view. No therapy known to modern medicine is 100 percent effective; all have a failure rate. Moreover, one can never predict ahead of time whether a therapy will work or not; one tries it and sees. Prayer is not unlike drugs and surgery in this respect. Sometimes prayer works, sometimes it doesn't; one never knows in advance. But, since controlled studies show that prayer statistically has a positive effect in bringing about greater healthiness in a variety of living organisms, why not use it? Why bury prayer in the grave of false hope?

I have long suspected that many critics who condemn prayer as false hope dislike prayer for personal reasons that they do not feel free to discuss or that they are not even aware of. Perhaps they had disappointing experiences with prayer early in life, which is very common. Such experiences often lead to antipathy toward religion in general. These attitudes may be understandable, but they are not becoming to a scientifically oriented physician.

In deciding whether or not prayer represents false hope, we should keep in mind the following facts:

- *Prayer works.* More than 130 controlled laboratory studies show, in general, that prayer or a prayerlike state of compassion, empathy, and love can bring about healthful changes in many types of living things, from humans to bacteria. This does not mean prayer *always* works, any more than drugs and surgery always work but that, statistically speaking, prayer is effective.

- *Hope heals.* Faith helps mobilize a person's defenses and assists in getting well, and optimism leads generally to better outcomes. Hundreds of case histories and scientific studies affirm this observation. As a single recent example, psychiatrist Thomas Oxman and his co-workers at Dartmouth Medical School investigated the role "religious feeling and activity" might play in 232 patients over fifty-five years of age undergoing cardiac surgery. Their finding: Those who derive at least some strength and comfort—hope!—from religion are more likely to survive longer after cardiac surgery than those who do not.

- *Hopelessness kills.* Numerous studies in humans show that we can die as a result of dire beliefs and a sense of overwhelming futility.

There is a spectrum of hope. At one end, hope *can* be false—for example, the saccharine, sunny prediction that the heart attack patient will be out of bed tomorrow or that the cancer patient will dance a jig by sundown. At the other end of the spectrum are the dismal predictions of doom that are out of keeping with the actual situation. (Physicians call such doomsaying "hanging crepe," as in the old custom of hanging black crepe at a funeral.) Neither end of this spectrum is appropriate; both are probably unethical. The best place to stand is somewhere in between.

But where? Which end of the spectrum will we choose to emphasize in dealing with sick persons? Even if we try to be neutral, the sick individual *perceives* hope or negativity in our behavior, words, and demeanor. There are no formulas to follow. Each individual, every physician, when dealing with illness, must find her or his own place to stand in hope's spectrum.

Fortunately, the "problem of hope" is more of a problem for doctors than patients. In my career as a physician, I have heard a great many complaints about "false hope," but all came from doctors, none from a sick person. During illness, most individuals are able to make a reasonably accurate appraisal of where they stand. Somehow they seem to know what lies ahead, and they are not likely to be taken in by breezy optimism or false hope. Their "bullshit detector" (a phrase I first heard used by theologian-psychologist Sam Keen) usually works rather well.

I have been asked many times by relatives and friends of sick and dying patients how they should behave when they visit their loved one in the hospital. Should they emphasize hope? Should they be upbeat? Almost always, words don't matter. The sick person needs love, not chatter. So, to those who fret about false hope: Don't worry. If offering hope troubles you, offer love instead. Nobody is troubled by "false love." Love, like hope, heals. It is the very foundation of prayer. If we allow hope to mingle with love, the "problem of false hope" will evaporate.

PRAYING FOR OTHERS
WITHOUT THEIR CONSENT

We do not feel that we need permission to *love* another person. Can we not *pray* for others without their consent, if our prayers are motivated by compassion and love?

We consider some types of human behavior to be beyond reproach: providing food and shelter, rescuing someone in harm's way, helping the sick and dying. Offering loving prayer is similar.

I have discovered, however, that there are rare individuals who are adamantly opposed to prayer. One such person I know is an extraordinarily brilliant man who values intellectual prowess above all. He believes our noblest task in life is to apply the power of reason to the problems that confront us and to live as courageously as possible. He despises what he calls the false comforts of religion. Not only is he convinced that prayer is worthless, he believes it is a cop-out, a refusal to deal squarely with our problems. In the end, he insists, we must save ourselves; no imaginary god will do it for us. When he discovered that a friend was praying for him, he was furious and angrily confronted her. Prayer, he charged, is a condescending, arrogant way of inflicting one's views on another. How *dare* his friend presume to know what was best! He ordered his friend to keep her prayers to herself.

There is a curious irony to protests like these. If the objecting man really believes that prayer is ineffective, why is he concerned that it will intrude in his life? Ironic or not, the concerns of those who do not wish to be prayed for bring the question of consent to the foreground. How should we proceed in this delicate area?

Two factors have influenced my own thinking on the question of consent. One, already mentioned, is love. The other is urgency.

Imagine that you are vacationing with your family at the Grand Canyon. You are standing on the rim, awed by the majestic grandeur of the endless vistas. Suddenly you notice that your dearest friend has ducked under the protective guardrail and is blithely strolling toward a one thousand–foot precipice. In this situation you would act as quickly as possible to snatch your friend from danger. Never would you pause to obtain his or her consent.

Many situations involving prayer are equally urgent— the loved one who has just been in an auto accident, the spouse who is having a heart attack. Praying for others in these instances is an immediate, reflexive action. We pray without reflection and do not bother with consent. But

prayer convincing. Before he prays for his patients he gives them a written statement of his wish to do so but adds that he will pray for them only if they have no objections. If a patient declines his offer, Dr. Rippo removes that patient's name from his prayer list. His system works beautifully. Almost all of Dr. Rippo's patients are exceedingly grateful that he would want to pray for them, and it is rare that patients decline his prayers.

The issue of prayer and consent requires treading carefully in sensitive and complex territory, as the following case shows:

> Several years ago my friend's husband, Stephen, was involved in a near-fatal auto accident and sustained serious injuries. We immediately marshaled several prayer chains in our church and other churches as well. His surgeons were astonished that he survived the operations to save his life, calling his response a miracle. As the man's recuperation continued, so did our prayers. But although he had been a successful businessman and ideal father and community leader, things were not the same. He seemed to have lost his vitality and zest for life. He was apathetic, as if he didn't care. He

was argumentative, grouchy, and hard to tolerate. This was a complete change from his previous jovial self. He was indifferent to his wife and children. Nothing seemed right.

Ten years later he died of natural causes. By the time he died, I had developed a practice of sitting in meditation for twenty minutes each morning. Several days after Stephen's death I was startled in my meditation by his presence. He stood in front of me laughing—his previous happy demeanor—and said, "I finally won out over all of you." And then he was gone.

As I pondered this, I could come to only one conclusion. Stephen hadn't wanted to live or perhaps hadn't been meant to live. But the power of all those prayers for his recovery had brought him back.

Stephen's accident and our prayers for his survival happened long before most of us had gained awareness of the power of thought and the importance of our choices. After that meditation experience I became much more conscious of the images I held and the words I chose in intercessory prayer.

There is a form of prayer that avoids most of the problems of consent. If we simply pray "Thy will be done," "May the best outcome prevail," or "May the highest good obtain," we are not inflicting our personal wishes on another. We are invoking a wisdom greater than our own without telling the world what to do. This form of prayer has been called a *nondirected* prayer strategy, in contrast to the *directed* method, in which the pray-er asks for a specific outcome. Experiments comparing these different prayer strategies show that they *both* work. One *can* make a difference through prayer without dictating the outcome.

"Thy will be done" prayers, offered with love, are one of the best approaches to praying without consent.

USING PUBLIC FUNDS FOR PRAYER RESEARCH

I realize using public funds for prayer research is controversial, but it is not as controversial as it might seem. Over 90 percent of people pray, and the overwhelming majority appear to favor public funding of prayer research. Most of them say, "This is a wonderful use of taxpayer money, compared to how my taxes are usually spent." I feel people should be informed about this debate, which is certain to achieve much notice in the future.

In 1992 Congress created the Office of Alternative Medicine within the National Institutes of Health. The mission of the office includes evaluating unorthodox therapies that show promise, and it focuses on three questions: Do these therapies work? Do they have side effects? Are they cost effective? The Office of Alternative Medicine does not perform original research; it evaluates and funds studies proposed by outside investigators. In order to be considered for funding, a proposal must have scientific merit.

One such study was proposed by Scott Walker, M.D., of the University of New Mexico Medical School in Albuquerque. Dr. Walker designed a study evaluating the effect of distant, intercessory prayer in a program of drug and alcohol rehabilitation. This was a double-blind study in which neither the health care team nor the participants in the program knew who was and was not receiving prayer. Would the prayer make a difference? Would those being prayed for do better than those just treated conventionally? (As of this writing, the results of Dr. Walker's study are awaited.)

In 1994, when the Office of Alternative Medicine released a list of the studies it had funded, the attention of the media focused on the University of New Mexico prayer study. Most of the major American television networks asked permission from Dr. Walker to dispatch camera crews to Albuquerque to "film the prayer in action." To his everlasting credit, Dr. Walker, like a good scientist, dismissed them. He simply said, "Let me do the study first; come back later."

When news of the study got around, criticism erupted. One of the most vehement objections came from the Freedom From Religion Foundation in Madison, Wisconsin. This organization wrote a letter to Secretary Donna Shalala of the Department of Health and Human Services, decrying the fact that federal tax dollars were being spent to evaluate prayer and demanding that this never be allowed to happen again. This was a violation, they maintained, of the constitutional separation of church and state. Secretary Shalala and her department offered no formal reply. But the incident was reported by a major newspaper wire service and appeared in newspapers around the country. Annie L. Gaylor, spokesperson for the Freedom From Religion Foundation, said, "If I knew my doctor was praying for me, I'd get another doctor. I'd rather they believe in medicine," implying that physicians can't believe in both and that agnostics make the best doctors. Gaylor denied that any evidence supporting prayer's effects exists, apparently unaware of the rich body of experimental findings in this area.

Dr. Walker and his colleagues at the medical school responded by stating they were not promoting prayer or religion. If any technique or therapy affects human health, they maintained, medical science should study it. They pointed out that federal funding has long been used to study the health-promoting effects of religious practices in general, including prayer. They were investigating a therapy that had appeared promising in other studies. Their experiment was not new.

The debate over public funding of research on the health effects of prayer continues. Critics seem generally to be poorly informed about the data that has accumulated in this area over decades, which strongly suggests that prayer is good for health. Strange alliances have formed among those opposed to investigating prayer scientifically. Those who object to the funding of prayer studies on constitutional grounds have joined with religious groups who believe it is heresy to "test God" in the laboratory. Into this fold have come a few scientists who are skeptical about prayer and who believe in principle it should not be studied. To bring together such divergent groups, prayer must be very powerful indeed!

This sort of opposition is not new. When Benjamin Franklin invented the lightning rod in colonial America, religious fanatics vehemently opposed it. It was wrong, they claimed, to divert lightning from the houses of sinners, to which God had directed it as a form of punishment. Lightning rods, therefore, were blasphemous; they contravened the will of the Almighty. The religious objectors were not persuaded by the obvious fact that the lightning rod could also be used to protect the dwellings of the righteous, which included, presumably, their own.

When the scientific evidence supporting the health effects of prayer becomes better known, resistance will diminish. While this debate continues, serious scientists are continuing to study the health effects of prayer quietly, out of the public eye. As they do so, those who oppose these developments need not worry excessively; almost all these studies will be funded privately, not publicly. And when the data is in, we shall see, if past studies are a guide, that prayer works—and that prayer, like lightning rods, can be used on behalf of believers and doubters alike.

MEDICAL MALPRACTICE AND
THE FAILURE TO USE PRAYER

In May 1995 the *Journal of the American Medical Association* published an article entitled, "Should Physicians Prescribe Prayer for Health?" This article described the steadily increasing evidence that religious practice, including prayer, is correlated with increased physical health. The appearance of this information in *JAMA* is prophetic; it indicates that more doctors than ever before are confronting questions about prayer in their medical practice.

Profound questions are being raised by these developments. If the evidence favoring prayer is valid, as many experts believe, are physicians justified in ignoring it? If prayer works, how can we physicians justify not informing our patients that prayer may help?

I faced this dilemma in my own practice of internal medicine. After encountering scientific studies supporting prayer, I became increasingly impressed by this body of information. I asked myself, Should I be using prayer on behalf of my patients? I decided that *not* doing so was the equivalent of withholding a needed medication or surgical procedure, and I began to pray for my patients daily.

Will we reach a point where physicians who ignore prayer will be judged guilty of malpractice? Malpractice has no absolute meaning. It is defined legally according to the standard of medical care that prevails in a given community. Because standards vary, malpractice is a shifting concept and differs from place to place.

What if most of the physicians in a given area become convinced that prayer is effective and begin to recommend it to their patients? Would this mean that their colleagues who do not follow this new community standard are guilty of malpractice? Perhaps not, because of the tendency to view prayer as a religious, not a medical, intervention. But this view may change as the scientific evidence supporting the physical benefits of prayer become better known.

Prayer *is* a medical and scientific issue. Today over 130 controlled scientific studies investigating the effects of intercessory prayer have been carried out, and over half of these show statistical evidence that prayer has a significant effect. In addition, more than 250 studies show that, on average, religious practice that includes prayer promotes health. An increasing number of physicians are learning about this body of data through articles like the one in the *Journal of the American Medical Association*, mentioned above, and through various books. Landmark conferences are taking place, such as the "Spirituality and Healing in Medicine" symposium at Harvard Medical School in December 1995 organized by Dr. Herbert Benson, a pioneer researcher in prayer.

As more and more conferences and scientific papers emphasize the latest findings in this area, the standard of medical care in our society may be reshaped to include prayer as a legitimate, scientifically valid intervention. What happens when the recommendation for prayer becomes the norm? Will physicians who don't recommend prayer be guilty of not meeting the standard?

As with almost all therapies, *referral* may also be a key concept in how prayer is used. As an internist, I'm not expected to perform brain surgery on my patients, but I am expected to refer them to a qualified neurosurgeon. It is the same with prayer. A physician may choose not to pray for her or his patients. But if the use of prayer is standard in that doctor's community, the physician can refer patients to outside sources for prayer, such as ministers, priests, hospital chaplains, or community prayer groups. In doing so, such a physician has met the obligation to the standard of care in her or his community.

When we take prayer seriously in medical practice, other legal issues may arise. Should physicians pray for their patients without consent? Is unsolicited prayer an invasion of privacy (see pages 53–59)? How can we prevent zealous, white-coated physicians from inflicting their private religious beliefs on their patients and evangelizing them in the guise of prayer?

There is another side to the question of malpractice and prayer—not the failure to use it but the decision to employ it. In an article in the *Wall Street Journal* on the scientific testing of prayer, Richard J. Goss, emeritus professor of biology at Brown University, says, "If my doctor prayed for my recovery, I'd consider a malpractice lawsuit." It might be difficult to win such a case. As we've noted, malpractice is defined according to the standard of medical care in a given community. If approximately half of American physicians pray for their patients, as shown in a recent survey by the National Institute of Healthcare Research, there appear to be shaky grounds for suing a physician because he or she prayed for a patient. If prayer is the norm among physicians, it would not appear to be malpractice.

How commonly would patients be upset to learn that their doctor prayed for them? It probably would be infrequent. In one survey, more than 75 percent of patients believed that their physician should address spiritual issues as part of their medical care. A full 40 percent wanted their physician to actively discuss religious issues with them. Nearly 50 percent of hospitalized patients wanted their physicians to pray not just *for* them but *with* them.

In spite of these trends, some physicians will prefer not to become involved with prayer, choosing neither to refer their patients for prayer from others nor to use it themselves. Perhaps patients who share these views will be attracted to such doctors. Will "prayer-free medical practices" arise in the future?

As the debate continues about the place of prayer in medicine, let us bear in mind that nothing can *make* physicians like prayer. Prayer that is demanded, required, and enforced lacks the genuine love and empathy that are its fire. If a physician wants to pray for a patient, that patient is fortunate, but all the attorneys and malpractice codes in the land are powerless to create a place for empathic prayer in the heart of a physician if it is not present already.

It is not greater legalization, but sacralization, of medicine that we need most.

WOULD YOU WANT A DOCTOR WHO PRAYS?

I once required an operation for a herniated disc in my back that had incapacitated me and was causing immense pain. When simpler measures did not work, I chose surgery. In selecting my surgeon, I weighed several factors. My primary criterion was the surgeon's technical skill and experience, not his or her private religious beliefs. I was more concerned about whether the surgeon was board certified in the practice of neurosurgery than skilled in the practice of prayer. I thought, "You handle the scalpel; I'll handle the prayer."

It isn't necessary for prayer to originate with the person wearing the stethoscope. We can pray in place of the physician, and we can recruit outsiders—relatives, friends, ministers, priests—to do the same.

A recent survey by Dr. David B. Larson and his colleagues at the National Institute for Healthcare Research in Rockville, Maryland, found that 43 percent of American physicians pray for their patients. How do you know your physician isn't one of them? Many doctors pray silently and in solitude. It seems they take literally Jesus' instructions to "enter into the closet" when praying, and they believe these prayers are as effective as those uttered at the bedside.

Prayer is making a comeback in medicine, and as it does so it will become easier to find physicians who are professionally expert and who also believe in prayer. Until then, how should we proceed? If you can find a physician who is technically skilled and who also prays for his or her patients, so much the better. But if you are faced with choosing either a praying physician whose professional skills are questionable or a nonpraying physician who is technically superb, my advice is to choose the technically gifted physician—and do the praying yourself. If you have a brain tumor and there's only one neurosurgeon around, it's probably not a good idea to mark her off simply because she doesn't pray.

When we need medical care, most of us want our physician to be of one mind with us religiously. But we ought to be careful that we do not place excessive religious demands on the physicians who serve us. We should recall that great healers have existed in cultures that worshiped gods different from ours; among them were Hippocrates, the legendary Greek father of Western medicine, and the great Persian physician Avicenna. Clearly, one can be a magnificent physician and not pray to a specific god—or perhaps not pray at all. I know agnostic and atheistic physicians who are superbly skilled, who care deeply for their patients, and who are loved by those they serve. I also know physicians who pray by the clock but whose patients can hardly abide them. Just as healing skills are not limited to physicians graduating from one particular medical school, they are not confined to those belonging to a particular religion or to those who pray.

As a patient, I would prefer a physician who prays, all things being equal. But since things seldom are equal, I would prefer a highly skilled, atheistic surgeon who swears like a sailor to one who never misses church but is heavy-handed in the operating room.

If prayer alone made good physicians, we could shut down the medical schools tomorrow. Something tells me we ought to keep them open.

PART THREE

WHAT IS PRAYER?

THE UNIVERSE IS PRAYER

No one knows when or where prayer began. Almost two thousand years ago Plutarch, the Greek biographer and historian, was struck by this fact. He observed, "If we traverse the world, it is possible to find cities without walls, without letters, without wealth, without coin, without schools or theatres: but a city without a temple, or that practices not worship, prayers and the like, no one has ever seen."

Scientists often try to explain the origins of prayer by applying the concepts of evolutionary biology. According to evolutionary theory, those traits and behaviors that help an organism survive and reproduce are perpetuated through time. In the long run, good visual acuity, speed, and muscular coordination win out over bad vision, slowness, and clumsiness. The fact that prayer survived through the long course of evolution suggests that it, too, may have conferred an advantage on the pray-er; otherwise it would likely have fallen by the wayside long ago. What was the advantage prayer offered?

Human beings, the speculation goes, experienced the urge to pray when they found themselves in a hostile environment where hunger and death were ever-present facts of life. Needing help, they began to look beyond themselves to imagined spirits and fantasized gods. Prayer thus had its roots in fear and desperation. Skeptics claim that we pray today for basically the same reasons. Whether we pray for healing or to win the lottery, we're still looking for help outside ourselves, just like our ancestors did.

But if prayer were only fantasy and self-delusion, why is it still with us? Why wouldn't it simply die out through the long march of evolution? No problem for the evolutionist. If one prays and is convinced help is on the way, one is likely to try harder to actualize the desired outcome. Fantasy or not, prayer reinforces our own efforts and encourages us to make things happen. Those who pray, therefore, have an edge in the high-stakes game of survival. And, since any behavior that confers such an advantage tends to be perpetuated, prayer is still around.

As tidy as this reasoning appears, the theories of evolutionary biology run into trouble. Biologists have no explanation whatever for the *distant* or *nonlocal* effects of prayer. They know ahead of time these phenomena *can't* happen, because the mind cannot escape the confines of the brain and body. The problem is, these events *do* happen. When put to the test in scores of experiments in modern laboratories, prayer works nonlocally, at a distance.

But the biologists are right up to a point. Prayer *does* give the praying person an advantage. But the advantage is not found just in "trying harder" to make one's desires come true, although this may happen to some extent. Prayer actually enlarges the reach of human consciousness. It is a way for us to transcend our physical limitations—to be nonlocal, like gods.

The capacity of consciousness to function nonlocally, at a distance, as in distant prayer, almost certainly did not originate in humans. Animals and birds can know at a distance. For instance, there are carefully documented accounts in which lost animals have found their owners across hundreds or thousands of miles, traveling to precise destinations they have never before visited. These cases are unexplainable by "homing" theories, hypotheses involving solar or stellar navigation, or by magnetically sensitive crystals in the brain. The capacity of these creatures for nonlocal ways of knowing may also be a form of prayer, a capacity that humans also use when we engage in intercessory or distant prayer.

Might the roots of prayer extend even deeper into nature than humans, animals, and birds? Could the roots of prayer extend to matter itself? The most profound experimental evidence within the whole of science for the existence of nonlocal events is in the subatomic domain. If one separates two electrons that have once been in contact and positions them far apart from each other, a change in one is associated with an immediate change in the other. The distance is arbitrary; they could be stationed at opposite sides of the universe. The electrons do not "talk" to each other, because the changes are instantaneous, meaning that there is no time for a signal of any sort to be transmitted between them. Therefore, the distant particles behave as if they are in some sense one, united as a single whole. This may be the most fundamental kind of "reaching out" ever identified—becoming so intimately connected that the two entities resonate completely with each other, no matter how far apart.

Is the outward reaching of subatomic particles a form of prayer? If so, the entire universe is prayer.

There is an old saying: "If you want to hide the treasure, put it in plain sight." If the nonlocal, outward reach of subatomic particles is a type of prayer, then prayer is all around and in us. We are suffused with it, down to the atoms and elements that make up our bodies; we eat, drink, and breathe it. Prayer is not just something we do, it is what we *are*.

Can we open our eyes to the treasure?

PRAYER IS AN ATTITUDE OF THE HEART

One of my best friends, Anne, is five years old. Her parents are quite religious and take her to church a lot. As a result, Anne is a pro about prayer, and she has become one of my favorite informants on spiritual issues. Sometimes she teaches me more than I bargain for.

During one of our chats she raised a profound question. "Larry," she asked, "why is prayer so *noisy?*"

Anne's query sent me back to the drawing board. What *is* prayer, and why do we generally believe it is connected with talking? The "talking view" of prayer usually begins in childhood with grace before meals and with "Now I lay me down to sleep" at bedtime. By the time we are adults, prayer has become noisy. Over the years, our concept of prayer incorporates not just the assumption that prayer involves words, but many other features as well. It usually evolves into something like this:

> Prayer is talking aloud or silently to a white, male, cosmic parent figure who prefers being addressed in English.

There are dreadful problems with this concept of prayer, in spite of the fact that most people in our society hold it. For one thing, Jesus and the founders of Christianity did not speak English. Neither were the founders of any other of the major world religions fluent in our tongue. And what about gender? Many people who pray do not address a male image but rather address Goddess. What about assigning personal attributes to our concept of the Almighty when we pray—assuming, for instance, that the Divine is "listening"? Millions reject any form of a personal god to whom prayers could be addressed. An example is Buddhism, which is not a theistic religion. Buddhists pray not to a personal deity but to the Universe. And they pray incessantly, twirling their prayer wheels as they go. Is Buddhist prayer counterfeit? Do Buddhists "really" pray? Although many fundamentalists insist that non-Christian prayer is inauthentic, it would come as a shock to Buddhists to be told their prayer is the wrong kind. And why do we smuggle race into our concept of prayer? Most people on this Earth who pray are not white, and they presumably do not envision the Almighty as Caucasian. For millions, the anthropomorphic, highly personalized image of the Almighty is hopelessly jejune. They may be drawn instead to a sense of universal order, majesty, and beauty or a sense of cosmic sacredness and majesty.

Back to Anne's question. Is prayer a form of talking? Must it involve words? A woman wrote to me, "I feel a deep desire to pray, but I cannot bring myself to use words. They seem unnecessary and silly." Oscar Wilde had similar doubts about words. He once wrote, "I do not talk to God so as not to bore him."

In its simplest form, *prayer is an attitude of the heart*—a matter of *being*, not doing. Prayer is the desire to contact the Absolute, however it may be conceived. When we experience the need to enact this connection, we are praying, whether or not we use words.

That doesn't mean words are wrong. People are often inspired to express verbally their unity with God, Goddess, the Divine, the Universe, the Absolute in some way—to lift their voices in words or song. If we need to use words, we should use them. But the essence of prayer is not something you say on Sunday morning, before meals, or at bedtime. The essence of prayer bypasses all the "Our Fathers" and "Hail Marys" and goes beyond all the *thees* and *thous*.

Anne was onto something important: Prayer need not be noisy. As an attitude of the heart, it can be invisible, silent, still. As Thomas Merton, the Catholic writer and monk, said, "I pray by breathing."

Following Anne's lead, we can expand the definition of prayer:

Prayer is communication with the Absolute.

This definition is deliberately broad. It allows people to define *communication* any way they see fit. It also invites them to image the Absolute in their own way—including the idea that the Absolute is both transcendent and immanent, "out there" as well as "in here."

In prayer, people may fill in the blanks any way they choose.

PRAYER IS WHAT IT NEEDS TO BE

A surgeon who was chairperson of his department at a major medical center said to me, "For much of my life I thought I did not believe in prayer. I felt I had left it behind when I went to college and medical school, but I realize I was wrong. I have been praying for my patients all along, every time I perform surgery."

He went on to describe his way of praying. For him, prayer involves a genuine feeling of compassion and empathy, which he extends to his patients before he enters the surgical suite. These feelings create a feeling of unity in which he feels bonded not only with his patient but also with all the other members of the surgery team. Against this backdrop he is filled with a sense of meaning and purpose, and he knows the operation will be more than an exercise in technique.

"Why did you feel you had given up prayer and that you weren't praying?" I asked.

"I grew up associating prayer with words and talking," he said. "Prayers were something you said, mainly for the purpose of getting something. Prayer was a verbal exercise in selfishness. This was a real turnoff, and I wanted nothing to do with it."

He went on to describe how his ideas about prayer had changed. "During surgery I feel totally immersed in what is happening. The more difficult the surgery, the more intense the feeling. Sometimes I feel as if the scalpel, the patient, and I are completely connected as a whole. This is often associated with a sense of reverence. I can't describe this—it's beyond words. For me, this entire experience is prayer—not something I do or say, but something I *feel*."

The surgeon was on target. Prayer often goes beyond words. But verbal prayer is not always inappropriate. If moved to do so, we may shout our word-prayers from mountaintops; we may adorn those words with music to form hymns, if that is what we feel. Language is a magnificent gift; why not use it in prayer?

We are not all superbly skilled with words. We should be grateful for this; life would be insufferable in a society where everyone was an orator. It is only natural, therefore, that we humans express ourselves differently in prayer— some relying more, some less, on language.

Is prayer words? Silence? Prayer is what it needs to be. When it erupts from us, we ought to allow it to follow the course or channel most natural to its flow. Problems arise when we erect blocks and dams—when we insist, for instance, that it should always be verbal, silent, wordy, musical, ritualistic, playful, or serious. When we fence prayer in, we fence people out—people who, like my surgeon colleague, felt that he was not praying because his form of prayer did not fit the religious norm.

A PRAYER FOR PRAYER

May we let prayer be.

May we allow it to follow
    the infinite patterns of the human heart.
May we learn to practice the most difficult art,
    the art of noninterference.
May we be guided by prayer
    instead of attempting to guide prayer.
May we allow prayer to be what it needs to be,
    to be what it is.

May we let prayer be.

DISTINGUISHING BETWEEN
RELIGION AND PRAYER

It is possible to pray without being religious, and one can be religious and not pray.

Prayer and religion are often confused, because in all cultures they are interwoven with formal rituals and ceremonies. At its simplest, however, prayer does not require cathedrals, churches, priests, or ministers. Prayer is and has always been a matter of the heart—a person's attempt to communicate with the Absolute.

But religion can empower prayer, and the need for ritual and ceremony, like the need for prayer, is deeply ingrained in human nature. Perhaps that is why, as Benedictine monk Brother David Steindl-Rast says, people are drawn to religion "inevitably." For most people, religious affiliation is a complement to prayer and exists naturally alongside it.

There are fundamentalists in every religion, however, who believe that one cannot engage in "true prayer" without being a member of their particular religion. This claim can be easily disproved. As we have seen, prayer can be tested in the laboratory under stringent experimental conditions to see whether or not it works. When the prayers of individuals from a variety of religions are put to the test, it is apparent that the prayers of many religions work. In fact, *there is no correlation in the laboratory between one's private religious beliefs and the outcome or effectiveness of prayer.*

A key factor in the effectiveness of prayer seems to be love, not the religion that accompanies it. As we have noted, this provides a way for Christians who believe in "the one true God" to accept the fact that the prayers of a variety of religions work. Christians believe God is love. If love is critical for the prayer experiments to work well, may not God be present in all of them? Thus, Christians might see the presence of God in all prayer, not just their own. This would allow them to affirm their own tradition while avoiding condemning the prayers of others.

THE BODY DOES NOT DISTINGUISH BETWEEN PRAYER AND MEDITATION

Both prayer and meditation come from the heart, and there are more similarities than differences between them.

Compare, for example, the practice of repeating the name of Jesus or Mary during Christian prayer with the custom of repeating a mantra, a word with special meaning, in certain forms of Buddhist prayer. During both of these practices one is often filled with a sense of serenity and a connection with something greater—whether *greater* is conceived of as God, Goddess, Buddha, the Universe, or the Absolute.

In the 1970s Dr. Herbert Benson, a specialist in cardiovascular medicine at Harvard Medical School, studied how the body responded to certain practices—Christian prayer, transcendental meditation (TM), biofeedback, hypnosis, and relaxation techniques called autogenic therapy and progressive relaxation. He discovered in all of them that the body showed a common response, which he called the Relaxation Response. It consisted of a lowering of the heart rate, blood pressure, and breathing rate; a reduced need for oxygen; less carbon dioxide production;

and so on. Benson found that, although our intellects may differentiate between prayer and meditation, our bodies do not.

Are there differences in the power of prayer and meditation when put to the test? Many experiments in prayer have been done in the past three decades involving people from various religious persuasions. They have included people of various faiths, including born-again Christians, devotees of Eastern religions, meditators of different persuasions, even agnostics. During the experiments, people are invited to use any psychological strategy they choose in order to accomplish the task at hand, which is usually to increase the healthy function of humans or nonhuman organisms. These studies show not only that a broad variety of individuals can accomplish this task but also, as we have already seen, that there is no correlation between one's private religious affiliation and the effect of the mental strategy.

It is people and prejudice who drive wedges between religious practices like prayer and meditation. Our bodies are wiser and less dogmatic.

ORDINARY MAGIC

People throughout history have regarded prayer as a way of acquiring things. If the Divine cares for our welfare and answers our prayers, will we be showered with gifts?

> Is a Mercedes Benz and a well-stocked portfolio a sign of God's grace? The Scriptural argument is uncompromising when it comes to the difficulty of the wealthy entering the kingdom of heaven and the nature of "filthy lucre" as the root of all evil. However, 70 percent of the heads of households surveyed by the Lutheran Brotherhood, a financial concern, said they considered their financial situation to be a reflection of God's regard for them. 49 percent of them said they prayed regularly for increased wealth.

Television evangelist Robert Tilton sees no limit to the Almighty's largesse. "That's right!" he exudes, without the slightest irony. "You can actually tell God what you would like his part in the covenant to be! . . . Step One: Let God Know What You Need from Him. New Car. New Job. Fitness. House. Finances." And last, and one wonders whether least, "Salvation."

The unexpected outcomes of selfish prayers are fertile fodder for jokesters and cartoonists. Here is one showing the Almighty's disdain for our selfish wishes:

> God pulls a man out of the cosmic cooker where he has been incubating, awaiting his next reincarnation. The man comes up talking. "Look. This time around I want a four-day-a-week job, a salary of fifty dollars an hour, health benefits, a retirement plan, two months vacation a year, good potential for promotion, and . . ." God lowers him back into the cooker and says, "Not quite done."

Novelist Aldous Huxley was exceedingly critical of how we badger the Almighty with our selfish prayers. He observed,

> To acquire the knack of getting his petitions answered, a man does not have to know or love God. . . . All that he requires is a burning sense of the importance of his own ego and its own desires, coupled with a firm conviction that there exists, out there in the universe, something not himself which can be wheedled or dragooned into satisfy-

ing those desires. If I repeat "Thy will be done," with the necessary degree of faith and persistency, the chances are that sooner or later and somehow or other, I shall get what I want. Whether my will coincides with that of God, and whether in getting what I want I shall get what is spiritually, morally or even materially good for me are questions which I cannot answer in advance. Only time and eternity will show. . . . The third clause of the Lord's Prayer is repeated daily by millions, who have not the slightest intention of letting any will be done, except their own.

Huxley was correct: We can be exceedingly devious in using prayer to get what we want. For example, one man reported that as a teenager he prayed for a car. When he did not get it he realized God did not work that way. So he stole a car and prayed for forgiveness instead.

"The just man loves God for nothing," Eckhart said. And when we set asking aside and allow love and gratitude to surface in our prayers, the results can be impressive, as in the following clinical story involving physician Betsy MacGregor of New York City's Beth Israel Hospital:

There was a seventeen-year-old boy who had been in a disastrous motorcycle accident. He had multiple fractures and ended up with . . . an infection of the bone . . . with draining fistulas in his leg. The surgeons carved out pieces of his bone and . . . flesh . . . trying to cut out his infection until finally he had a cavity in his thigh that you could put two fists into.

. . . He was in tremendous pain when the orthopedist came to change his dressings every day. I found him to be a whimpering, cowering person who was just preoccupied with his fear and pain. As I began to do something about his pain and help him both with medication and some relaxation techniques . . . we got to talking about what his dreams and hopes were . . . before the accident.

. . . I asked him did he pray to God, and he said, yes, he was begging God to heal him. I told him there might be another way to pray to God rather than pleading, that he might say to God that it was really important to be healed. Finally, after a couple of months, he said to me one day, "You know, I really prayed to God differently these last few days.

I have been saying I really need to be healed, God. I'm not just begging You to heal me. I need to be healed because there are things I need to do, and it's really important that You help me heal." And this young man said it in such a different way, it was really amazing. He said it out of a place of strength in himself, rather than out of anxiety and despair. He left the hospital with his infection cured and his wound healing, a totally different person than the whimpering, apathetic person I first met.

Frequently a blessed paradox occurs when we ask for material things. We may not get what we ask for, but in the failure to receive what we request, we often receive a greater gift. This is illustrated in the "Prayer of an Unknown Confederate Soldier":

I asked God for strength that I might achieve;
I was made weak that I might learn to obey.

I asked for health that I might do great things;
I was given infirmity, that I might do better things.

I asked for riches that I might be happy;
I was given poverty that I might be wise.

I asked for power that I might have the praise of men;
I was given weakness that I might feel the need of God.

I asked for all things that I might enjoy life;
I was given life that I might enjoy all things.

I got nothing that I had asked for,
but everything that I had hoped for.

Almost despite myself my unspoken prayers were
    answered;
I am, among all men, most richly blessed.

Were our prayers for material things denied? The experience may help us focus more keenly on what we already have—a life composed of magical events wrapped up in small moments. How could anything material add to the splendor of the here and now? When we realize that every moment is in some sense already perfect, our gaze may cease to wander ahead, as it often does when we pray for some better future. We may learn to dwell with gratitude in the moment—and to know with Margaret Bonnano that "it is only possible to live happily ever after on a day-to-day basis."

Prayer is not about getting. It is about being mindful of the moment and perceiving the magic in the mundane.

As writer Adair Lara says, "And some, like me, are just beginning to guess at the powerful religion of ordinary life, a spirituality of freshly mopped floors and stacked dishes and clothes blowing on the line."

Prayer helps us appreciate the dazzling simplicity of ordinary life. As the Buddhist aphorism reminds us, "After ecstasy, the laundry."

PART FOUR

HOW TO PRAY

—ɯ—

CREDENTIALS DON'T MATTER IN PRAYER

Prayer is an activity anyone can successfully engage in, regardless of whether you are praying for the first or the millionth time. But are some pray-ers more skillful than others? There are two schools of thought.

In a careful experiment performed at the University of Iceland in Reykjavík by professor of psychology Erlendur Haraldsson, a skill factor was identified in healers who uniformly use prayer. The study assessed the ability of seven individuals to affect the growth of yeast cells in test tubes. Of the seven participants, three were engaged in healing (two were spiritual healers and one a physician who practiced spiritual healing). The other four subjects were students with no experience or particular interest in healing. A total of 240 test tubes were used, 120 receiving the healing intention, with 120 as the controls. The test tubes were placed in front of a subject who tried on several occasions, for ten minutes each time, to increase the growth of the yeast in the liquid by the mental method of his or her choice. The individuals were not allowed to touch the tubes or come closer than one foot. After twenty-four hours, the growth of the yeast was measured in each test tube by a light absorbency calorimeter read by a research assistant who did not know the controls from the treated tubes. In addition, another experimenter made independent measurements. The researchers concluded, "The results indicate that mental concentration or intention (spiritual healing) affected the growth of the yeast." Analysis revealed that there were fewer than two chances in a hundred that the positive results could be explained by chance. The bulk of the positive scoring was done by the three healers. When their scores were analyzed separately, there were fewer than four chances in ten thousand that the results could be due to chance, whereas the student-nonhealers gave chance results.

In a series of experiments performed by Spindrift, a prayer research organization, the skill factor was assessed by asking people of varying prayer experience to try to influence the germination rate of seeds and the metabolic activity of yeast cultures. In these tests, as in the Iceland experiment, the more experienced practitioners produced the more powerful outcomes. These studies indicate that practice, interest, and experience make a difference in spiritual healing, which for most healers is based in prayer.

Why *shouldn't* there be a skill factor in prayer? Prayer involves a focused state of mind usually characterized by feelings of internal quiet, serenity, and stillness. Anyone who has ever tried to still the mind knows how agonizingly difficult this can be. Saint Teresa of Ávila compared the attempt to achieve this mental condition to trying to ride a bucking horse. Buddhists call our ordinary psychological state "monkey mind." But practice makes perfect; the more we engage in prayer and meditation, the quieter the mind becomes.

Experiments in prayer suggest that love is one of the most important factors influencing its effectiveness. In healing, it underlies the sense of oneness with the patient that is experienced by the healer. Most people learn how to love across the course of a lifetime. Does not this suggest that the effect of prayer might vary as our capacity for love deepens? And what about the consistency of our love? There is an old saying, "Love is like bread. It has to be made fresh daily." Perhaps learning to pray means simply learning to love—deeply and dependably.

The contrasting point of view is that the prayers of everyone are equally effective and that no skill factor exists in prayer. Reflecting this point of view, a woman wrote to me,

> It is wrong to imply that experience makes a difference in prayer. Prayer is a level playing field. When

we pray we are all the same. Coming from the heart in love and sincerity is the only thing that counts. We should avoid setting up a hierarchy in prayer, with priests and ministers on top and the rest of us on bottom. That's not what prayer is all about. If you stress the role of experience in prayer, this will discourage novice or first-time pray-ers from taking up this practice. We should be *encouraging* people to pray, not turning them off.

I do not believe these two points of view are mutually exclusive. A skill factor exists in practically all human activities, from cooking to billiards to making love. To say that a skill factor exists in these areas does not prohibit anyone from participating in them. Anyone can pray, no matter what their level of training may be. The important thing is to begin.

Everyone agrees that a genuine prayer must come from the heart and be sincere. This suggests that individuals who are new to prayer may be more effective than prayer veterans, because their experience is fresh and new to them, not rote and habitual.

The Bible tells us straightforwardly, "The prayer of a righteous man availeth much." It does not say, "The perfectly executed prayer of a righteous man who is highly experienced in these matters availeth much." Prayer is for novices as well as veterans.

It is conceivable that a prayer from a single, sincere person might avail more than a million casual, thoughtless prayers. Or that the heartfelt prayer of a first-time pray-er might outperform that of a master pray-er who was having a bad day. If I were sick I would enlist the prayers of people I love and who love me. I would want compassionate, empathic individuals on my side. I would not be concerned whether they've prayed for fifty years or whether they took it up yesterday. In prayer, compassion, love, and caring—not credentials—matter most.

CHILDREN ARE PRAYER

Walt Whitman wrote in *Leaves of Grass* in 1855,

> There was a child went forth every day,
> And the first object he looked upon and received
> with wonder or pity or love or dread, that object
> he became,
> And that object became part of him for the day or
> a certain part of the day . . . or for many years or
> stretching cycles of years.

Whitman saw that children do not pray; they *are* prayer.

If prayer is "communication with the Absolute," as we have proposed, the communication lines for children seem always open and humming. While the rest of us labor to get through, young children seem to experience no struggle, no barriers to overcome. Children have an unobstructed relationship with the Infinite.

The child is the metaphor for spiritual purity the world over, and "become as a little child" is one of the most universal elements of spiritual instruction. The goal in our prayer life, however, is of course not literally to become a child, but to become *as* a child by embodying the innocence and genuineness of the child in our adult prayers.

This distinction may seem obvious but it has been greatly misunderstood. Many twentieth-century thinkers, including Freud, believed that religious impulses represent an urge to regress psychologically to an infantile, childlike state. For him, all mystical experiences of unity and oneness were simply a reversion to the oceanic, undifferentiated form of perception of the infant, in which "self" and "other" are indistinguishable. The mystical urge was just a disguised yearning for the crib, cradle, and breast. This view, although it still enjoys great popularity among hard-nosed skeptics, confuses *regression* and *progression*. All valid spiritual experience, including the ecstatic, higher reaches of prayer, is a march forward to maturity, not a reversion to infantility. As anyone who has entered a path of spiritual discipline knows, the spiritual life is not for wimps. It is hard work. To suggest that this path can be traversed by infants or by infantile adults is plain nonsense.

No one stays a child, nor should they. The diapers and dependence must go. This is true physically *and* spiritually. The challenges and suffering that are part of growing up add breadth, depth, and a richness to life that the child does not know. These experiences bring about a toughness and resilience without which life cannot be lived.

Today, when our world appears so chaotic and unmanageable, many people look longingly to the simplicity and innocence of the child. One expression of this is the public's fascination with angels, which often take the form of infantile cherubs and beatific, androgynous, winged children. We should remember that angels, in addition to being innocent and pure, can also be stern, no-nonsense, tough-minded beings who take no guff from anybody. They are not just cuddly, airborne babes. Angels carry swords of fire. Cupid's arrow hurts. As the poet Rilke said, "Every angel is terrible."

Our longing for the lost innocence of the child can also be seen in the popular school of psychotherapy called "inner child work." The inner child represents the early stage in life when nurturing and love are mandatory if healthy psychological life is to follow. Traumas at this stage may lead to emotional problems later on. By contacting these painful experiences through deep relaxation, guided imagery, or hypnosis, many people are able to neutralize these pathological effects and find greater peace in the present. But many therapists who employ

—꿈—

these techniques have noticed that some people not only *contact* their inner child but, having made contact, hang on for dear life. These people want to luxuriate endlessly in the blessed state of childhood, where the needs for physical security and emotional support are provided by someone else. Skilled therapists know how to nudge forward people who get stuck at this stage. They are able to help their clients become *as* a child and not remain a child.

Children are icons of innocence. They are prayer incarnate because their communication with the Absolute has not yet broken down. They remind us of what we once were and what we may realize once again.

FOUR-LEGGED FORMS OF PRAYER

The effect of prayer is not restricted to humans. Prayer has been proved to work on practically every living thing to which it has been applied—humans, various cells and tissues, animals, plants, and organisms such as bacteria, fungi, and yeast. The evidence supporting these widespread effects is abundant and includes more than 130 controlled laboratory studies, as we've mentioned.

Some people have difficulty accepting these experiments because they can't imagine how one could possibly pray for bacteria or other so-called lower forms of life. How could one experience enough empathy and love for these nonhuman creatures to genuinely pray for them? For millions of animal lovers, this is not a mystery; for them, animals are simply not "lower." Some religions, such as Hinduism, view nonhumans with the same reverence we extend to our own kind. This degree of reverence for life is not just "Oriental." I'm reminded of a very old saying from Jewish mystics: "Over every blade of grass bends an angel whispering, 'Grow! Grow!'"

Researchers have begun to study the health benefits of having pets. These studies have interesting implications for our understanding of prayer. Aaron H. Katcher, a physician at the University of Pennsylvania School of Veterinary Medicine, and his colleagues found that 98 percent of dog owners spent time talking to their dogs, 75 percent thought their dogs were sensitive to their moods and feelings, and 28 percent even confided in their dogs. Katcher believes people derive benefits from these interactions not unlike those from prayer. "Without being irreverent," he states, "it is possible to think about the similarities of the comforts of prayer and the comforts of talking to an animal. Prayer is frequently accompanied by sensual enrichment such as incense, music, special body postures, the touch of folded hands or rosary beads, just as dialogue with an animal is accompanied by the enrichment of touch, warmth and odor. In both instances the talk is felt to be 'understood.'"

Devotion to a pet, like devotion to prayer, can bring about improvements in human nature, as seen in the dynamics of families. Ann Ottney Cain, professor of psychiatric nursing at the University of Maryland in Baltimore, studied the sociological impact of animals in sixty families who owned pets such as dogs and cats as well as more exotic skunks, goats, and monkeys. She discovered that many of the families experienced increased closeness, more time playing together, and less time arguing after they had obtained their pets. "One woman even used the family's dog to cool family arguments," Cain reports. " 'Stop fighting, you're upsetting the dog,' was her favorite comment."

Harvard University's Dr. Herbert Benson showed in the 1970s and '80s that prayer can reduce stress and lower blood pressure and heart rate by inducing what he calls the Relaxation Response. Dogs may be a four-legged form of prayer, because they bring about the same effect. Being in their presence results in a lower blood pressure, researcher Katcher discovered. Dogs don't have a monopoly; gazing at a tankful of tropical fish lowers blood pressure, too.

Prayer breaks down barriers between people. So, too, do pets. Peter R. Messent of the Animal Studies Centre in Leicestershire, England, recruited eight dog owners and asked them to take two strolls through Hyde Park— once with their dog and once without. An observer followed, recording the responses of the people who passed within five feet of the walker or the dog. There were a significantly greater number of responses, and more longer conversations, if the dog owners were with their pets. It did not matter if the dogs were pedigreed or not.

Being around pets, like praying, brings out compassionate behavior in people. Sharon L. Smith studied interactions between ten pet dogs and their family members. She found that the pets provided men as well as women a socially acceptable outlet for touching—rubbing, scratching, patting, or stroking—something that American men are reluctant to engage in.

And pets, like prayer, save lives. In a study of ninety-six people with heart disease released after treatment at a coronary care unit, psychiatrist Erika Friedmann of the University of Pennsylvania in Philadelphia and her co-workers discovered a higher survival rate one year after hospital discharge among pet owners, even after accounting for individual differences in the extent of heart damage and other medical problems. In fact, Friedmann's team found that having a pet at home was a stronger predictor of survival than having a spouse or extensive family support.

To summarize, there are striking similarities between prayer and having a companion pet. These include:

• Having someone to talk to

• Developing compassionate behavior

- Fostering a sense of being welcomed or greeted

- Promoting a sense of being loved unconditionally, "no matter what"

- Reducing psychological stress

- Increasing health and saving lives

- Breaking down barriers between people

At Riverside Methodist Hospital in Columbus, Ohio, one of the most valuable members of the hospice staff is Barlow, a handsome golden Labrador. Barlow makes rounds with the nurses and physicians and enjoys immense rapport with patients. At Maine Medical Center in Portland, another beautiful Lab, Pandora, makes regular rounds in the intensive care unit with her handler. Pandora is quite photogenic, and the staff nurses report that she adores being photographed—a real camera hound. "Pet Therapy Program Guidelines" have been adopted by the hospital's physician and nursing staff, and the program enjoys enthusiastic support by patients and personnel alike.

Can animals pray? Because prayer involves a sense of love and connection and a reaching out, perhaps the answer is a qualified yes. If so, might "animal prayer" have healing effects? Most authorities would ascribe the positive influences of pets to psychological factors such as stress reduction from having a pet around; proposing "pet prayer" is going too far. Yet many pet owners would not find it outrageous to suppose that their unconditionally loving Lab is extending prayerlike healing influences to them.

Why take an anthropocentric attitude toward prayer? Why would the Absolute limit prayer to *Homo sapiens*? Pet prayer, if proved, would be yet another step in the democratization and universalization of prayer.

The next time I get sick, I plan to get on the prayer lists of as many Saint Bernards as I can.

A DOCTOR TESTS PRAYER

In 1994 the beloved fourteen-year-old dog of Dr. Hilary Petit, a veterinarian in Sacramento, California, developed a severe problem. She could not stand on her own and had to lean against a wall or fence to walk. Dr. Petit feared the diagnosis was recurrent cancer. Four years earlier her dog had undergone the surgical removal of one eye because of a cancer growing behind it. The tumor had been incompletely removed, and the dog had received radiation following surgery. Had the cancer regrown and spread, causing the current problems? In case an ear infection might be contributing to the problems with balance and walking, Dr. Petit treated her dog with a course of antibiotics. Other treatments included Dramamine, steroids, and thyroid supplementation, to cover other possibilities. All failed. In fact, the steroids seemed to aggravate her problems.

Dr. Petit, by then desperate, describes what happened next. "One night, at my wit's end on how to treat her, I remember just asking for ANY help, any help at all, either in helping her recover or deciding that it was time to euthanize her." She then experienced one of the biggest surprises in her career as a veterinarian.

The day after I . . . asked for some help . . . she took several steps without leaning against the fence. The next day she took about twenty steps before drifting back against the fence and walked from my car to my apartment (about a hundred yards) without my having to do more than correct her drift a little. . . . She had been unable to walk unassisted for about at least six weeks. . . . Throughout that day she navigated the apartment with only occasional "rebounds" off the walls—about every four to six steps she would drift off to the wall—then would correct her own path.

Paradoxically, Dr. Petit was not jubilant about her beloved dog's improvement.

The sad part of this story is that I have to admit that I pretty much scared myself with this. I could not reconcile her recovery with my medical training—partly because it was so rapid and dramatic, and partly because I had withdrawn all treatments except the prayer. I am sorry to say that the third night (after the second day of recovery) I elected not to renew my prayer, out of consternation and confusion about what appeared to be the consequences of praying. The next day my dog relapsed and her condition continued to deteriorate rapidly, and in fact I euthanized her about two weeks later.

Dr. Petit was willing to acknowledge and confront her own fear about these events.

The things that continue to stay with me are these: (1) I would have done anything (at the time that I began praying for her) to help her; thus, I think my usual restrictions about what is and is not possible, acceptable or "allowed" in terms of response to prayer were temporarily suspended; (2) I had a distinct experience of disbelief in and rejection of her recovery ("this can't be happening") even as I was overwhelmed with delight in her improvement; (3) in my struggle to reconcile the traditional, left-brain, scientifically trained piece of my mind with the radical, unexplainable, and totally unscientific recovery in front of me, I did feel some sense of fear, a sort of "what have I done?" reaction, and some rejection of the idea that I had somehow brought this on by my actions; and (4) even though I tried (naturally) to repeat the remission by further prayer once she began to deteriorate again, I was never as wholehearted about it because I was afraid to find out that I could, by the simple expedient of prayer, somehow effect such a completely unexplainable and outrageous result.

Dr. Petit was changed by these events.

As a consequence of this complete disarrangement of my previous locked-in-dogma medical thinking, I have begun trying little prayers on little things. For instance, [while performing surgery] in spays where a uterine horn stubbornly eludes my efforts to fish it out, I've begun doing a sort of "C'mon, God, help me out here" prayer, and so far that produces the uterine horn every time on the first or second try afterwards. . . . There are other [examples]. At the very least, this experience has given me a great deal to think about, such as how best to apply this information to the benefit of my patients. . . .

While I had essentially no religious or spiritual upbringing, I have been fascinated by spiritual and "paranormal" subjects all my life. . . . However, despite considerable exploration and investigation, I have been much more accepting of the possibility that *someone else* could do these things than that I could. It's okay for *you* to be able to perform incredible and unexplainable miracles; I can be completely serene in accepting that. But for whatever reason I am very uncomfortable with the thought that *I* might mediate the same act. I realize that's not rational; and since the death of my darling dog I've begun to seriously rethink that, since I am fairly certain that had someone else's prayers resulted in her recovery or had she recovered for unknown reasons, . . . I would have accepted it without reservation.

I have immense faith in the capacity of physicians to deal with their fears of prayer. Doctors are trained in science, which is a method of suspending judgment and setting aside prejudice. Dr. Petit's experience illustrates how a skeptical physician might respond to prayer. After she recovered from the shock of her encounter with the outrageous, she began like a good scientist to conduct her own experiments by "trying little prayers on little things." This is exemplary behavior—neither uncritical acceptance nor wholesale rejection, but openness in the face of the unknown.

When we confront the workings of prayer we confront the infinite, and it is natural to recoil from something so much greater than ourselves. But we must go *through* the fear we feel at such moments, and not around it. If we do, the fear can change to become our ally and our strength: the infinite in service of the finite.

OVERCOMING AMBIVALENCE
AND CONFUSION ABOUT PRAYER

"Many a Christian prays faintly, lest God might really hear him, which he, poor man, never intended," C. S. Lewis once said. Fear of results is one type of negative thinking about prayer. There are many others.

Millions feel that prayer is drudgery, but they do it anyway because they fear punishment if they don't. Others feel guilty or selfish about praying for themselves. They seem to sense that Emerson was right when he said that most prayer was an exercise in meanness and theft. Some people feel that prayer is downright arrogant: Who am I to tell the Universe how to behave? Many of our ambivalent attitudes toward prayer stem from childhood. Prayer, we learned, usually involves talking aloud or silently, usually at some length, to a wizened, no-nonsense male god who is listening intently to make sure we get it right and that we pray on schedule. No wonder we are ambivalent about prayer!

Negative attitudes toward prayer are often unconscious, because we tell ourselves that prayer is a good thing and we ought to enjoy praying. Unable to confront these negative feelings, we repress them into the unconscious part of the mind, where they continue to frustrate us when we pray.

Professing to love what we dislike, of course, is not limited to prayer. Millions of people exercise vigorously and eat sensibly, hating every minute of it. Orson Welles once said that there is more virtue in a man who eats caviar on impulse than in someone who eats Grapenuts on principle. The caviar eater is following his heart; the Grapenuts eater, his rigid sense of duty. So with prayer. The person who prays rarely but out of heartfelt desire is expressing greater genuineness than someone who prays compulsively by the clock.

When we do acknowledge our ambivalent attitudes toward prayer, we often fall into self-reproach: "If only I were more spiritually mature, I wouldn't feel this way!" The result is often to try even harder to "like" prayer. This approach doesn't work because it reinforces the negative attitudes one is trying to resolve.

Four steps can help us resolve our negative attitudes toward prayer:

- *Stop taking our prayer life so seriously.*

    When I find myself taking my own prayer and meditation too seriously—feeling as if I should be more disciplined and "pray better"—I remind myself that I am still learning. I also keep two sayings at hand that invariably help me lighten up and put things in perspective: G. K. Chesterton's observation, "Anything worth doing is worth doing badly," and the old witticism, "How do you make God laugh? Tell him your plans." Comments such as these can remind us of something we often forget: The Universe doesn't depend on whether or not we get it right in prayer.

- *Realize that negative attitudes toward prayer are universal.*

The saints and mystics of all the great religions have grumbled about prayer from time to time. Like us, they found it difficult to stay on track in prayer, and they lamented their weakness. Confessing his shortcomings during prayer, John Donne said, "I throw myself down in my chamber . . . and invite God and his Angels hither, and when they are there, I neglect God for the noise of a fly, for the rattling of a coach, for the whining of a door."

If we sometimes feel like failures at prayer, we are in good company.

- *Remember that there are many types of prayer and a great many ways of praying.*

  If we're having trouble with one method, we should explore others. If "asking" prayers—prayers of petition and intercession—do not feel appropriate, we might consider focusing instead on other types, such as prayers of adoration, celebration, or thanksgiving. For most people, these prayers feel lighter. They can help us resuscitate our prayer life when it is in the gutter of joyless duty.

- *Recall that prayer is not just a matter of* doing *but also a way of* being.

  As Dorothy Day put it, "Does God have a set way of prayer, a way that he expects each of us to follow? I doubt it. I believe some people—lots of people—pray through the witness of their lives, through the work they do, the friendships they have, the love they offer people and receive from people. Since when are words the only acceptable form of prayer?"

  Prayer can take the form of prayerful*ness*—an attitude, a state of mind in which we feel a sacred connection with the Absolute. Prayerfulness bypasses the bowed head and the bent knee and all the *thees* and *thous*. It exists not just in church but also while mowing the lawn or washing dishes or driving kids to soccer practice. Through prayerfulness we can help heal our negative attitudes toward ritualized, formal prayer. In prayerfulness, sacred feelings arise naturally from the depths of our being, like a clear spring surfacing on a mountain slope. Prayerfulness can lead us back, full circle, to prayer, but prayer transformed, prayer that is as spontaneous and natural as the dawn.

WHO CAN BENEFIT FROM PRAYER?

In the experiments dealing with the effects of prayer in humans, researchers found that intercessory prayer was effective even when the recipient *did not know* he or she was being prayed for. In addition to studies in humans, many experiments show also that a variety of lower organisms (bacteria, fungi, yeast, seeds, rats, mice, and various types of cells) can be made healthier through prayer. These creatures presumably do not *know* they are being prayed for. They presumably are not religious and do not "believe" in prayer.

One often hears that we must "let prayer work" if we are being prayed for. Yet, the prayer experiments indicate that intercessory prayer is effective even when the recipient is unaware of it. This means that we cannot consciously control the effects of prayers being offered on our behalf.

The effect of prayer, however, can be strengthened by belief. This is true in many areas of life, including modern medicine, where doctors make positive use of belief all the time. When a physician gives a patient a medication and strongly implies that it will be effective, this sets in motion actual physical effects due to suggestion and expectation—the placebo response. These positive effects appear to enhance whatever the medication does. So it is with prayer: Its effects are strengthened by belief and faith.

So much for the recipient. What about the pray-er? If I am praying for you, must I believe my prayer is going to work? Many experiments in prayer and prayerlike states of consciousness suggest that positive belief is vitally important. In the field of parapsychology, where people achieve distant effects with the mind, it has long been known that "sheep" (those who believe a distant effect is possible) are more likely to achieve greater results in experiments than "goats" (skeptics who do not believe in the possibility).

I personally feel that "unbelieving prayer" is a contradiction in terms. I don't see how anyone can genuinely pray while believing the effort is worthless.

Some people think *belief* and *faith* in prayer are the same, but they are not. Faith has been called "the substance of things hoped for, the evidence of things not seen" (Hebrews 11:1 KJV). Unlike faith, belief is generally based on things that *are* seen and that can be demonstrated. In my own life, the experimental evidence that prayer works when put to the test in the laboratory has created in me a strong *belief* that prayer works. My beliefs are based on empirical evidence, not blind faith. But my belief in prayer does not diminish my *faith* in it. There are many mysteries surrounding prayer that science has not illuminated and perhaps cannot illuminate—and yet I continue to have faith.

If your belief and faith in prayer falter, don't chastise yourself for your doubts. Above all, don't try to make yourself believe in prayer. Allow your beliefs to meander; don't force them; let them develop naturally. When it's time for you to believe more strongly in prayer, you will.

If you try to manufacture a belief, it will not be genuine. Psychologists speak of the "double bind," a no-win situation in which you are wrong no matter which way you turn. A classic example of a double bind is when a controlling parent gives the message to his or her little boy, "Darling, you *must* love me, because all good children love their parents!" The parent is requiring the boy to do something that is genuine only when it is not required, when it arises naturally. If he heeds the command, the love is not genuine and he has failed. But if he ignores the command and actually dislikes his father or mother, he has also failed. In either case he is a bad child—the double bind. An identical no-win situation arises when we tell ourselves that we must believe in prayer or else we are spiritual failures.

We should not be so serious about whether or not we believe in prayer. Prayer does not require our belief, as recipients, in order to work. We would do well to heed the teenage street wisdom to "lighten up" on this matter and to recall the observation of British writer G. K. Chesterton: "Angels fly because they take themselves lightly."

WHEN WE NEED TO PRAY, WE WILL

People often ask me, "Should I pray?" The way I see it, that's like asking if you should drink water or eat food. Breathe. Sleep. Make love. When you *really* need to do so, the question answers itself.

When children learn to walk, they do not first ask whether it is right to do so. They simply walk because it is natural. Normal children cannot keep from walking. Walking is simply what children do.

Prayer is as natural as walking. It is a mistake to worry too much about whether or not we ought to engage in it. Asking endless questions such as "Should I pray?" is what Buddhists call "putting legs on a snake." The legs are completely unnecessary and just get in the way. According to another Buddhist saying, "When walking, walk. When sitting, sit. Don't wobble!" In other words, don't be halfhearted. This is a valuable lesson for spiritual practices such as prayer.

Psychologist and theologian Sam Keen has warned about "spiritual stuttering"—putting an endless series of obstructions between us and our spiritual goal. One way to avoid stuttering spiritually is to pray when we feel we must, when it feels completely and totally right, no matter how frequent or infrequent this may be. In this way we can avoid the formulas and injunctions, which just get in the way.

A few years ago I was having dinner with Paulos Mar Gregorios, who was then president of the World Council of Churches. Across the table was a contentious young woman who was intent on picking an argument with him. Deliberately trying to provoke a confrontation, she proclaimed, "I don't believe in God!" Dr. Gregorios responded with a compassionate, loving smile, and said gently, "Don't worry. If you need to, you will!" Prayer is like that. When we need to pray, we will.

When prayer becomes a natural activity like walking, it is no longer a chore. When this happens it feels as if we are no longer praying but instead are being prayed. Saint Francis was said to be such a person—someone who did not pray but who was overtaken and enveloped by prayer. As Richard Foster said, Francis "seemed not so much a man praying as prayer itself made man."

Praying in a contrived way is like trying to breathe on purpose. Anyone who has tried to control her breathing finds soon enough that it works best if left alone. For some things to work best, we need to get out of the way.

But how far out of the way? Some spiritual masters have suggested that we step aside totally in prayer. As the Benedictine monk Brother David Steindl-Rast says, "As long as you know you are praying you are not praying properly."

Should you pray? If you need to ask, you've probably already begun.

THERE IS NO BEST WAY TO PRAY

It isn't morally superior to use one method [of prayer] over another; the right thing to do morally is to be honest. . . . What is right for one person isn't always right for another. People . . . should beware of being smug; . . . it will lessen the healing effect.

—*Deborah Rose*

When someone in an audience asked a famous theologian how to pray, she responded, "It's so simple. Ask God." This is one of the most important pieces of advice about how to pray: We must discover the method that is best for us. In prayer, no formulas exist; there is no best way; one size does not fit all.

"People ask, What type of prayer should I say?" reports Deborah Rose, former vice president of Spindrift, Inc., a research institution that has been investigating prayer for more than two decades.

Catholic, Protestant, Jewish, nonverbal? Shall I ask for something or just try to be open? . . . This is like asking, What kind of instrument should I play? Violin? . . . The harp? The piano? It depends on your individuality, your circumstance, your background, and your inclinations. What suits you? It is important to develop a prayer style . . . you are comfortable with. It is also good to keep in mind that the style in which you pray will change from time to time. When facing death people pray differently than they do when they pray in church or say grace. . . . What is important is the quality and harmony of the music. Not the instrument that produces it.

The studies I cite throughout the book not only show that prayer works, they also reveal clearly that there is more than one way to pray. A variety of methods are effective. One can pray for a specific outcome such as an increase in the immune system's activity. On the other hand, one can employ a general "Thy will be done" approach or simply pray, "May the best thing happen." One can use words or silence; one can pray at a distance or at the bedside. All these methods have yielded positive results when actually put to the test. There is even evidence that we can pray in our dreams. Therefore, although people throughout history have sought the one true way to pray, they have not succeeded, because a "prayer formula" does not exist.

This goes against our grain. In modern life we have come to believe overwhelmingly in experts who have the answers we need. In every category of human experience, consultants and specialists have sprung up like spring weeds. When we want solutions we commission a study, convene a panel, or hire a team of professionals. This belief in the knowledge of experts colors our assumptions about prayer. Surely, we tell ourselves, there must be people out there — ministers, priests, rabbis, saints, mystics — who know the best way to pray.

When it comes to prayer, we must be our own consultants. That does not mean we can't benefit from the observations and experiences of others. But at some point we must set their advice aside, plunge in, and discover our own unique approach to prayer.

What about the theologian's advice to "ask God" how to pray? This may sound as if a heavenly consultant is waiting to give us all the answers. But asking God does not mean looking outside ourselves "up there." When we ask the Absolute how to pray, we go *inside*, because if the Almighty is omnipresent, she also dwells within. As mythologist Joseph Campbell put it, "The kingdom of heaven is within. Who's in heaven? God! That means God is *within!*" By going inside ourselves we become our own high priests.

Philosopher and author James W. Jones relates a tale of ancient India that expresses beautifully the wisdom we each contain. According to legend, the gods were arguing over where to hide the secret of life so men and women would not find it. "Bury it under a mountain," one god suggested; "they'll never find it there." "No," the others countered, "one day they will find a way to dig up the mountain and uncover the secret of life." "Put it in the depths of the deepest ocean," another god suggested; "it will be safe there." "No," said the others, "someday humankind will find a way to travel to the depths of the ocean and will find it." "Put it inside them," another god said; "men and women will never think of looking for it there." All the gods agreed, and so it is said the gods hid the secret of life within us.

How should you pray? Don't worry too much about it. Set aside your ideas of right and wrong. Experiment with different methods, and be gentle and forgiving of yourself as you do so. When your prayer ritual feels awkward and clumsy, smile, pat yourself on the back, and pray anyway.

MORE PRAYER IS NOT ALWAYS BETTER

There's an old joke about a west Texas rancher whose cattle operation is in shambles because of drought and gutter-level beef prices. His herd is starving, his wells are dry, and beef prices continue to fall. It costs him more to market a cow than he gets paid for it. One day a neighbor rancher, who is in the same fix, comes by for a chat. Leaning on a fence post he says, "It can't get much worse. How are we gonna stay in business?" The old rancher confidently replies, "We're gonna do it with volume."

With prayer we often take the same approach. More must be better. So we try to smother our problems with volumes of prayer, as if prayer were some sort of celestial ketchup that can cover up all the bad flavors of life, if only we use enough. A glimpse at history should tell us we are off-track here. Numerous sickly, short-lived saints and mystics have existed who spent their lives in continual prayer, while many people who have never uttered a prayer never get sick and live to be a hundred. When it comes to prayer, more is not always better.

Sir Francis Galton, the eminent nineteenth-century English scientist, performed the first scientific study on prayer. He wanted to know if those who received the most prayer—royalty, heads of state, and high-ranking members of the clergy—lived longer. Even though these figures were awash in prayer, Galton found their longevity was not greater, and he concluded that prayer does not extend life. (His study, however, contained many flaws. Among them was the fact that the royalty was exposed to one of the greatest health hazards of the day—the constant attention of medical doctors. In addition, there may have been people who were praying *against* them as well, which Galton apparently never considered.)

What if prayer works like homeopathy? What if, contrary to reason, less is more? In that case we ought to be praying sparingly but very, very thoughtfully—praying seldom but well.

I am not advocating praying less instead of more; I am sure in some cases it is wiser to pray often. I am suggesting, however, that prayer abounds with mystery and that we ought to pay more attention to *how* we pray than to *how often*—quality as well as quantity.

Today many drug companies produce generic medications that are much cheaper than the brand-name products of the major pharmaceutical firms. But although the cheaper tablets contain the same amount of the active drug, in some instances they have been shown to pass through the entire length of the intestinal tract without ever dissolving. They emerge whole and unchanged, just as they were when swallowed. These pills are no bargain. You can consume them by the handfuls with no benefit whatever.

When we pray, do our prayers "dissolve"? Or do they remain as ineffective as when we uttered them? They may sound genuine—they may contain the right words, they may have been prescribed by spiritual authorities, they may even come from holy books or prayer manuals—but never become active.

We Americans generally believe that if we work hard enough and long enough we can overwhelm obstacles and achieve our goals. We often carry this idea into our prayer life. But with prayer, harder is not always smarter, and more is not invariably better.

What *is* better? Can we identify an essential ingredient in prayer that is necessary for it to work? In the scores of scientific experiments dealing with prayer and a prayer-like state of consciousness, one of the most crucial qualities appears to be *love*—compassion, empathy, deep caring. Love implies letting go, venturing outside the self, breaking down the boundaries separating ourselves from others. Other studies suggest that a particular kind of letting go is also important—a letting go of preferred out-comes. In these experiments, when people use a "Thy will be done" approach, in which one does not dictate terms but asks only for the greatest or highest good, prayer often seems more effective.

Love released: Without it, prayers don't dissolve.

CHOOSING TO PRAY PRIVATELY OR PUBLICLY
DEPENDS ON OUR TEMPERAMENT

Are you an introvert who prefers aloneness and solitude or an extrovert who prefers the company of others? Most of us have a predominant personality style or temperament, and these differences affect the way we pray.

Group or "corporate" prayer has definite advantages. It can feel good to congregate with others who share our beliefs, values, and purposes. On the other hand, many deeply spiritual people prefer to "enter into the closet" and pray privately, as Jesus commanded in Matthew 6:6.

The question of whether group prayer is better than solitary prayer relates to the question of whether more prayer is better. Is it better to combine our prayers with those of others and pray as a team? Some of the most interesting attempts to answer this question have come from researchers in Transcendental Meditation (TM). They have conducted several experiments in which the quality of life in a community—the level of violent crime, alcohol and drug consumption, theft, and so on— is assessed before and after the group meditation effort. These studies strongly suggest that more meditation indeed produces greater results.

I have long been fascinated by these experiments, which have been published in prestigious scientific journals. When I was invited to Maharishi International University in Fairfield, Iowa, where many of the TM researchers live and teach, I asked them, "If prayer and meditation work at a distance, as the research suggests, why do you need to come together in a group to achieve this effect?" "Because it helps us focus, and it feels good," was their simple and wise reply. The group process assisted their discipline of actually engaging in meditation. Being together elevated their mood and increased their energy. Anyone who has participated in group rituals realizes the good sense of these observations.

British theologian and physicist John Polkinghorne, president of Queens' College, Cambridge, has offered an interesting rationale for why group prayer may be wise. He invokes the metaphor of the laser. Laser light is unusually powerful because it is "coherent"; that is, all the crests and troughs of the waves making up the light are in step. "I believe that divine and human coherence in prayer . . . can make things possible which would not be so if we and God were at cross-purposes," Polkinghorne observes. "It is appropriate to encourage many people to pray for the same thing. That is not because there are more fists beating on the heavenly door, but because there are more wills to be aligned with the divine will"—more coherence, more order, more power, like the light of the laser.

Throughout history, instructors in prayer have long recognized that the differences in human temperament must be taken into account. Centuries ago, certain European prayer manuals distinguished between two forms of prayer, the way of Mary and the way of Martha. Mary's way was solitary, quiet, contemplative. It was a way of being, not a way of doing. In contrast, Martha's way was more active and public. It involved recitations, verbal exercises, and the use of specific images—a way of doing in addition to being. These prayer strategies reflected a keen understanding of different temperaments. They anticipated the concepts of introversion and extroversion, which were not introduced into modern psychology until the twentieth century by C. G. Jung.

Is private or group prayer best? Whether we pray publicly or in solitude depends on our temperament, our personality styles, our natural inclinations.

Knowing how to pray requires knowing who we are.

YOU CAN PRAY IN YOUR DREAMS

Throughout history people have often tried to pray during sleep and dreams. Consider, for example, Peregrine Laziosi, a revered Catholic priest who lived in Italy from 1260 to 1345. Peregrine developed an advanced cancer of his foot and was scheduled for an amputation. Amputations in fourteenth-century Italy were gruesome; the extremity would be sawed or cut off with a dull instrument while one was awake. Peregrine, not surprisingly, is said to have prayed before sleep for a healing to come to him in the night. He had a vision that he was cured. When he awoke the cancer was gone, surgery was canceled, and he spent the rest of his life ministering to people afflicted with cancer. He was canonized as Saint Peregrine in 1726 and is known as the patron saint of cancer patients.

This idea of unconscious prayer currently causes great difficulty for many religious people. After my book *Healing Words* was published, I was invited for an interview on a Christian television network that broadcasts via satellite throughout the world. Before the show the host took me aside to check what I was planning to say on camera. He knew I was not affiliated with any particular religion, and he was nervous about my views on prayer.

Was I interested in exploring any specific area? I responded that I was particularly fascinated by the role of the unconscious mind in prayer, particularly those instances in which healing comes during sleep, as in the experience of Saint Peregrine. I said that I felt viewers would be interested in this little-explored aspect of prayer. The host was horrified. He became ashen, and for a moment he was speechless. "Oh, no!" he finally managed to stammer. "We can't possibly discuss that!" I had stepped over the line into the domain of the unconscious. I respected the wishes of my host and did not discuss dream prayers.

Why do some religions have such immense distrust of the unconscious mind? They seem generally to believe that when we dream or when we meditate and "become empty," anything can happen, including invasions by evil in every conceivable form. Opening up the unconscious is an invitation to spiritual disaster, they think, and we must always be vigilant. (One wonders whether this point of view ever leads to sleep deprivation in the devout.)

These fears stem from some inaccurate assumptions, such as the idea that the unconscious is a complete blank. Anyone who has explored the unconscious knows it is hardly empty. It is highly alive; it never rests. Not re-alizing this, the religious objectors equate the uncon-scious with a defenseless, helpless state that makes us an easy target for an infinite variety of nastiness.

Negative attitudes toward the unconscious can also be found, of course, in the work of Sigmund Freud. For him the unconscious was the repository of pathological de-sires and repressed fantasies. Freud is widely regarded as one of the most formidable enemies of religion in the twentieth century. Distrust of the unconscious makes strange bedfellows.

In spite of widespread mistrust of the unconscious, many examples, such as that of Saint Peregrine, suggest that the unconscious mind may be intimately involved with prayer and healing. Perhaps this isn't surprising. During sleep and dreams we set aside our egos and our psychological defenses. As a result, prayer doesn't have to battle the skepticism and doubt that are present during our waking life. In dreams, anything seems possible, and miracles happen. Maybe this is why dreams often seem to be one of the most effective forms of prayer.

Prayers and dreams interact in an infinite variety of ways, as in the following experience:

In December 1992 I was diagnosed with an aggressive cancer of the urinary bladder that had spread to the lymph nodes. I went immediately to the Mayo Clinic for a second opinion. The Mayo physicians, like my original doctors, recommended immediate surgery—removal of the bladder and prostate—with which I complied. After my recovery, all the doctors were emphatic that I should take chemotherapy in case the cancer had not been completely removed surgically. I eventually decided against this recommendation, choosing instead to use several natural methods with which I was familiar and in which I believed.

The second night after beginning this program, I had a talk with God. I told him I was absolutely confident I was doing the right thing, that I was healed or would be completely healed, and that I wanted him to confirm this in a dream with a sign so obvious I could not mistake it.

Here's the dream: I was the passenger in a car traveling through the countryside. Looking out the window I saw a light suddenly appear in the sky, way up. It got brighter and brighter, lighting up the entire universe. I was excited and turned to the driver and said, "That's his light! That's the light they talk about in the Bible. . . . That's his sign!" I woke up knowing I had received his sign, that I was doing the right thing, and that I would be healed if I was not already.

I am totally and completely clean of all cancer. Even my skeptical oncologist could find no symptom or sign. I feel humble and blessed by these experiences.

Finding one's direction—knowing how to proceed in one's life—has come to people in dreams throughout recorded human history. Consider the following account:

Within two years, my husband and I had lost our jobs. With four children at home, life had become very difficult. For my husband, it was a career crisis. Unable to get another job, he was working on establishing his own business. For me, it was more of a spiritual crisis. I had spent the past three months since I lost my job on internal searching—reading, meditating, walking, thinking—longing to find direction to my next "life's work."

Then I had a dream. I was driving down a very dark freeway. There were no lights at all and no other cars on the road. Suddenly, in the distance, I saw the two bright headlights of a car coming toward me—in my lane! I had time to think and make a decision about the best way of avoiding a head-on crash. Though I knew it was customary to move to the right, I judged that, in this case, moving to the left was the better choice. I pulled off to the left, and as the car safely passed me, I said to myself, "Wow, I certainly hope he realizes he's going the wrong way and turns around." Very soon after I started driving again, I saw in the distance *many* bright headlights coming toward me. This time I realized *I* was the one who was going the wrong way! Again, I had time to think and make a decision. I quickly did a U-turn and safely drove away.

I thought about the dream when I woke up but applied no meaning or interpretation to it. Later that night, during my evening prayers, feeling insecure and uncertain, I asked for reassurance. As soon as I expressed that, I realized that my prayer for reassurance was answered! And I understood the message of my dream to be that I used to be

traveling in the wrong direction, but now I was
going the right way.

Can we actually cultivate dream prayer? Many contemporary researchers in the field of "lucid dreaming"
say yes. Lucid dreaming is a state in which one knows
one is dreaming, and it often involves the voluntary control of one's dream contents. Books by researchers Stephen
LaBerge, Jane Gackenbach, Robert van de Castle, and
many others are available to guide anyone interested in
exploring this fascinating area. Parapsychology researchers
Stanley Krippner and Montague Ullman have performed
laboratory experiments indicating that specific information can be acquired during dreams and can be purpose-
fully exchanged between individuals at a distance. This
research suggests that the contents of dreams are not the
random noise some scientists have suggested.

Throughout human history, dreams and night prayers
have served the great priests, shamans, and seers of every
culture. Most cultures have viewed dream events as gate-
ways to the gods. Even in the Bible, dreams were seen as
conduits of wisdom from the Almighty to humans. One
of the modern obstacles to these ancient customs is the

idea that prayer must always be a *waking* activity involving words, recitations, ritual, and attendance at a cathedral, church, or synagogue. Certainly these activities are part of prayer, but they are not the whole picture.

The thirteenth-century Christian mystic Meister Eckhart said, "There is nothing in all creation so like God as stillness"—including, we may presume, the stillness of dreams.

GLIMPSING THE INFINITE

One of the greatest burdens we carry is the certainty that life will end tragically in death. This fear rests on our belief that time flows, much like a river, and that it is carrying us irreversibly toward extinction. Death awaits everyone; nobody escapes the ravages of time.

In spite of the common feeling that time is a flowing, one-way process, no experiment in the entire history of science has ever shown that time flows. This comes as a surprise to many people, who assume that scientists settled the basic questions about time a long time ago. In fact, the nature of time is hotly debated within science, with no resolution in sight. Don't expect to get ultimate answers from scientists about what time is. Some researchers, such as Nobel Prize winner Ilya Prigogine, seek to restore linearity and direction to time, along the lines of common sense. Others, like Nobel Prize winner Richard Feynman, have declared that the nature of time is simply "too difficult," implying that we may be in the dark about these questions for a very long time to come. Physicist John Hagelin, an authority in an area within physics called string theory, believes that time isn't made of successive units such as seconds, minutes, and hours.

Rather, he states, "The only natural unit of time is Eternity."

Is life destined to end tragically in death? It depends on the answers we give to the nature of time. If time doesn't flow as we assume, perhaps we should take another look at the meaning of death. This is not to suggest that death does not happen but that its significance may be different from what we ordinarily assume. It may not be the absolute ending we think it is.

How can we decide? Instead of praying not to die, perhaps we might pray instead for a different understanding of time—time as eternity instead of a flowing process always pointing toward annihilation. If prayer provided us with such a nonflowing experience of time, it could neutralize our sense of tragedy.

Prayer *can* reveal what eternity feels like. During prayer we often feel that time stops, and for a moment we glimpse the infinite. This perception can extend beyond prayer to every waking moment. It is possible for this new way of being in time to become so real that we continually feel immortal. For those who have gained this awareness, immortality is not a theoretical possibility but a certainty. This is one way prayer annuls tragedy—not by preventing negative events from occurring, but by modifying the impact these events have on us by transforming our sense of time.

Rather than devoting time to prayer, perhaps we should devote prayer to time—not the flowing time from which our fears and anxieties are constructed, but time that is infinite and eternal.

Why can't prayer eradicate all the tragedy in the world? Perhaps it already has—just in time.

FORGIVING OURSELVES FOR GETTING SICK

"If only I'd been farther along my spiritual path, the biopsy would have come back negative," one of my patients once said. Why do we blame ourselves for getting sick? I call this New Age guilt, and it is currently epidemic in our society. The accusations can also come from others. I call this New Age blame.

Sure, disease *can* be a reflection of the psyche. For example, people who experience a tremendous degree of psychological stress at work and have no control over the demands of their job have a higher incidence of heart attacks. Also, it is well known that individuals who are burdened with a sense of stress and anxiety and who are cynical and angry toward life in general—the so-called Type A personality—are more likely to die younger of heart disease.

But examples such as these do not mean that *all* diseases are correlated with psychological problems or spiritual failure. Many great saints and mystics died from dreadful diseases, sometimes at a young age. As theologian Karen Armstrong observes in her book *Visions of God*, "Mysticism can have serious health threats. The mystical life should carry a health warning: it can seriously damage your mental and physical health." If "being spiritual" immunized one against illness, the saints and mystics should have been healthy and long-lived. The fact that they often were not shows that one can attain great spiritual heights and get very sick.

Why did the cells in the stomach of Ramana Maharshi, the most beloved saint of modern India, become cancerous, and why did this God-realized man die a painful death from stomach cancer? Why did the Buddha, the Awakened One, die from food poisoning? Why was Saint Teresa of Ávila afflicted with crippling arthritis? Or why did our biopsy turn out positive—in spite of the fact that we may have done immense spiritual work in our lifetime? In each instance, the cells in the body are just being themselves, doing what cells do, which sometimes involves malfunctioning.

In the past half-century, medical scientists have discovered the most intimate connections between mind and body. These insights, marvelous as they are, should not be extended too far. The correlation between mental and physical health is general, not invariable. Even if we do our spiritual homework, it is *not always* the case that we will be blessed with good health.

In the first verse of the first chapter of the book of Job we read, "Job . . . was . . . perfect." And later on, "In all this Job sinned not." Job's story shows that perfection, personal disaster, and physical illness can go hand in hand. Sometimes our body's cells are just going to be themselves and break down, no matter how spiritually advanced we may be.

Almost everyone experiences illness sooner or later. When we ask the inevitable questions—Why is this happening? Why me?—we should resist blaming ourselves for causing the problem. When our organs, cells, and molecules malfunction, rather than criticize them we might thank and bless them for sustaining us as faithfully as they have.

Gladys McGarey, M.D., former president of the American Holistic Medical Association, is a physician who understands the value of a forgiving, lighthearted attitude toward the body. She once stated that women ought to be less morbid about doing breast self-examinations. Instead of searching for breast lumps with fear and trepidation, she advises women to actually address their breasts as good friends when beginning their exam: "Hi girls! How are you? What's going on today?"

We ought to take a less demanding attitude toward our bodies. Our bodies might be grateful. Nobody likes to be told they have to be perfect all the time.

PRAYING "THY WILL BE DONE"

Using a "Thy will be done" or "May the best thing happen" approach in prayer requires faith and trust that the best outcome will prevail. It also means setting aside our preferences and demands. This can be very difficult, because most of us feel we know in advance what's best, and we waste no time in telling the Absolute what to do.

That's why many of us have a hidden agenda when we use an open-ended form of prayer. If we have an illness and pray "Thy will be done," we often catch ourselves thinking, "By the way, I wouldn't mind if the illness went away." Or, "Thy will be done, but send me a job promotion while you're at it." If our personal demands and wishes contaminate our "Thy will be done" prayers, the prayers are not sincere.

One of the best reasons to rely on an open-ended, nondirected prayer is that our knowledge is limited. Even when we think we are praying for what's best, we may be misguided. Deborah Rose, former vice president of Spindrift, Inc., a prayer research institution, gives the analogy of praying for healthy tomato plants. We assume that the best thing for tomato plants is to produce lots of bigger, redder tomatoes, and to do so fast. But is this really what's best? Tomatoes of this type can be produced by putting the plants in a hothouse, but tomatoes grown this way do not taste as good, they reproduce more poorly, and their resistance to disease is diminished. Therefore, although we thought we were praying for healthier plants, we discover that this type of prayer is actually unhealthy for them.

Might it have been wiser simply to pray "Thy will be done"? If we had done so and the tomato plants had grown more slowly and produced fewer and smaller tomatoes than we desired, we may have complained that our prayers were not answered. But they indeed may have been answered from the standpoint of the tomato plants.

Rose believes the Spindrift research points to an "ordering force" in prayer, which prevents prayer from being used to stimulate an organism beyond what is good for it. When dairy farmers prayed "Thy will be done" in a Spindrift experiment, their cows gave *less* milk, not more. Rose explains:

> The ordering force often causes a cow to give less milk because cows in America often are conditioned and bred to give more milk than is good for them. . . . People will say, "Oh my prayer didn't

work. The cow gave less milk." It did work. The ordering force is going to do what is best for the organism, not necessarily what you expect.

Sometimes the ordering force hypothesized by Spindrift researchers appears to consider not just the needs of the organism but the needs of the community as a whole:

> If you are starving and about to lose your farm and you prayed for the cows and you needed [them] to give enough milk so that you could raise the money to save the farm and feed the family, . . . the ordering force might result in a cow giving more milk, but it would do so in a way that wouldn't hurt the cow. . . . The ordering force works in the best interests of the community. It can't be manipulated or fooled, and it has its own innate ethics or system of justice. It will interact with the needs of the whole.

Spindrift continued to put these ideas to the test. Although their prayers resulted in less milk production by cows in the United States, prayers for goats in Haiti produced *more* milk. In Haiti, milk was sorely needed; in the United States, it was not. The researchers at Spindrift consider this an example that the ordering force in a

"Thy will be done" prayer does not act blindly but considers the needs of both the organism and overall society.

This may seem bewildering. What *are* the organism's needs? What are the needs of the community and the society at large? What is the balance between these? In a "Thy will be done" approach we do not need to know these answers. The ordering force provides them with no help from us.

While engaged in health work with rural people in Haiti, the Spindrift team had trouble storing milk. They therefore prayed for some sort of primitive cooling system to keep the milk fresh. Although the cooling system did not appear, the milk began to stay fresh several days longer without refrigeration. When they tried to replicate this result on returning to the United States, they were unsuccessful. "We don't know for sure [why the results were different]," Rose says, "but we think it has something to do with need. In my kitchen at home we did not really need the milk to stay fresh, whereas in Haiti lives literally depended on it."

If Rose's observations are correct—if the site of an experiment and the social context are important—the implications for science are profound. According to current scientific thinking, the place where an experiment is conducted is irrelevant. If an experiment works in Boston, it should work equally well in Brazil. While this may be true for certain kinds of experiments, it may not be true for studies involving prayer and other activities of consciousness. In order to accommodate how prayer works, scientific theory may have to be extended beyond its present framework.

I once received a letter from a man who charged that the "Thy will be done" type of prayer was a cop-out. "People without courage are attracted to this method," he said. "If people pray 'Thy will be done,' they can always say the prayer was answered. They never have to face the fact that prayer is worthless. If they had guts they'd pray for something specific, and risk seeing prayer fail." I disagree. A "Thy will be done" prayer strategy is not for cowards but for people who have the strength to accept the verdict of the Absolute, whatever it may be. It's much easier to make specific demands and requests. The greater challenge is to be content with less milk, not more.

PRAYING FOR CORN IN IOWA

Talk about a prayer list. The Reverend Karl E. Goodfellow, a Methodist minister in Guttenberg, Iowa, has twelve thousand on his. This is roughly the number of farm families in the eight counties that make up his church district in the northeastern part of the state. The Reverend Goodfellow thinks big. His list may soon grow to around one hundred thousand, the total number of farms in the state.

Goodfellow began doing prayer research as part of a seminary doctoral project. At that time he was interested in the social changes in churches that resulted from prayer. Later he discovered evidence suggesting that prayer can affect the germination rate and growth characteristics of seeds. When he became a rural minister in Iowa, where is found some of the richest farmland on Earth, he had a magnificent opportunity to test the effects of prayer on plants.

Goodfellow's church started praying for seeds, and the blessed seeds yielded better. Then he asked God to bless part of a cornfield. Farmers who participated in the experiment reported higher yields in the areas where the crops had been blessed. Farmers are practical people; when something works, they take notice. So, too, did the media. Goodfellow's project was featured in national publications, and he was invited onto talk shows.

Why the intense interest? In recent years, farm failures have occurred at an alarming rate throughout the American Midwest. With each farm closure, approximately $70,000 is lost to the local economy. The loss is not just economic. In Iowa, people realize they are tied to the farm whether they live in the country or not. The social fabric is being jeopardized by the dwindling farm population. People see neighbors disappearing, schools and churches dying, and entire communities being threatened.

Goodfellow began to discuss the problem with clergy throughout his area. Every minister he talked to shared his fears about the impact of the declining farming community. If prayer worked for crops, Goodfellow wondered, why not for farmers? He set a goal of finding a prayer partner for every farmer in Iowa. Prayer partners would pray daily from October 8 through November 30, the height of the harvest. He was surprised to discover that there were about one hundred thousand farms throughout the state. "It was a bit overwhelming," he said. So he scaled back the project to include "only" about twelve thousand families in the eight counties in his church district.

Each person who agreed to participate received the names of ten farm families for whom to pray, plus a booklet of devotional messages with a strong rural flavor. The farm families were prayed for daily, by name. Although some of the pray-ers preferred to pray anonymously, the parishioners doing the praying often sent a letter to the farm families on their list, together with a copy of the devotional booklet used in the project, if desired. "For a lot of farm families, the only time they are contacted by a church is for money," Goodfellow says. "This may be the first time they have been contacted to say that they are being prayed for, that they are appreciated for the roles they play in their churches, communities, and schools."

In addition to praying for a bountiful harvest, parishioners pray also for a reduction in farm accidents, which are a scourge in rural America. Farming is not only hard work, it can also be very dangerous. Missing fingers, hands, and arms are common sights on America's farms.

The booklet used in the Iowa project is *God's Harvest—God's People*, a grass-roots collection of inspirational messages written by northeastern Iowans themselves. The messages are touching. The Reverend Joann Hary, pastor of the United Methodist Church in Aurora and Lamont, who grew up on a farm, writes about her father's loss of an arm in a farm accident and his subsequent rehabilitation. Her father "made friends" with the appliance he wore for a left hand, and he would visit other injured farmers. He assured them that if by the grace of God he could make it, so could they. A few pages later Richard Shaw of Calmar tells about his heartache when he was forced to leave his farm. I felt moved as I read these messages of loss and faith.

I grew up on a small cotton farm in central Texas, and all my life I have had a deep respect for farm families. For all their hard edges, farmers can be some of the most spiritually inclined people I have ever met. In general, they have a sacred, reverential regard for the land. As I read some of the Iowan devotionals, I became even more convinced of these views.

"Respect the natural systems and cycles," urges the devotional for October 10, written by the Reverend Mary K. Green of the United Methodist Church of Edgewood, Iowa.

Know our surroundings and the needs. Use logic, ethics, and nurturing love, as any shepherd does. . . . The loss of topsoil is a threat to basic civilization. When topsoil is gone, so is the potential for life. . . . Farmers are called to feed 92 million more people each year with 24 billion tons less of topsoil each year! . . . . The future depends on non-damaging ways to farm. The fate of the earth's lands and waters is determined by how WE use them. EVERY person has a chance to act. Become physically, personally and spiritually tied to the land that sustains us. Be empowered by knowing your acts make a substantive, positive difference in God's creation. Set out to do the right thing, be the Good Shepherd, though it may be difficult, inconvenient, or costly.

Liz Goodfellow, whose husband is Karl, wrote the devotional for October 28. Liz also grew up on a farm, and she learned as a child that pain and suffering are never very far way on a busy farm.

Accidents happen so quickly. Anyway, it seemed that way when one second my brother threw the switch to operate the silo unloader and the next we saw blood dripping from my father's arm. He'd been trying to fix it, but when he yelled down the chute, we'd misunderstood his instructions. *Oh God, help. What had we done?* Thank God my father remained calm and kept his senses. He quickly told us what to do to help him and soon Mom and Dad were on their way to the emergency room. The rest of us stayed home to finish chores and wonder. Was he going to be all right? Why did this have to happen? Would we ever be able to help again? Our hearts sank into despair. We never meant for anything to go wrong. *Hear my cry, O God; attend to my prayer.* . . . Dad came home that same day, stitched up and smiling. . . .

Since the prayer project began, farmers have begun to report interesting experiences — "things that have happened that could have been disasters but weren't." One farmer was sucked into a gravity wagon of grain, which could have suffocated him, but he was pulled out unharmed. Another farmer near Hawkeye was driving a combine down the road when a semitrailer pulled in front of him. Only a "miracle" prevented what should have been a fatal collision.

Some people object to this approach to prayer. Praying for bountiful grain harvests, they claim, is selfish. Would those who object to praying for grain, to be consistent, also reject the Lord's Prayer, "Give us this day our daily bread"—praying for the bread that is made from grain?

Goodfellow's prayer project goes beyond more bushels per acre. He believes prayer helps not only the person or situation being prayed for, but also the person doing the praying. As a pastor, he saw that often when people prayed about the welfare of others, they became more compassionate themselves. They would take time out to make a phone call, pause to chat with someone on the street, or take food to someone in need. It is not surprising, therefore, that Goodfellow's prayer project has affected not just farmers but urbanites as well. The city folk seem to have grown closer in their understanding of farm folk, expressing their caring by writing letters and making phone calls to them. The farmers are grateful. One farmer said that at a time when it seems like so many people are against farmers, it was good to know that someone was supporting them. A farmer from Melville called to say, "You don't know me, but I just want to call and say thank-you. Every day we face a lot of pressures, and it's just nice to know that someone cares about us."

The Reverend Goodfellow has been swamped with requests for the devotional material and for advice on starting prayer networks. He is working with a group from the University of Iowa on collecting actual data about the effects of the prayer on the bounty of the harvest and the rate of farm accidents. He plans to expand the program to include all the hundred thousand farms in Iowa, then all the farms in the Midwest. Where will the funds come from? That, too, is on his prayer list.

THE ANSWER ISN'T ALWAYS YES

People often wonder why prayer isn't answered 100 percent of the time. But how do we know it isn't? There are many other perfectly good answers to prayer, such as *no, perhaps, maybe, not yet,* or *we'll see.* If we added up all the possible answers, perhaps our prayers *are* answered 100 percent of the time.

If we look at prayer from a medical point of view, we can ask, What therapy *does* work 100 percent of the time? No such therapy has ever existed. Even the most powerful treatments fail occasionally. Moreover, physicians never know ahead of time whether or not a particular therapy will work on a given individual. We simply weigh the chances, give it a try, and hope things work out, but as all doctors know, they often do not. So with prayer. We never know what the outcome will be, but we pray anyway.

It's a good thing that our prayers aren't always answered yes. For example, if all the prayers for curing disease that have been uttered in the history of the human race had been granted, almost no one would have died. This would have resulted in global disaster millennia ago through massive overpopulation. Today there would be no place to stand, and the Earth would be unfit for human habitation.

The fact is, we are not wise enough always to know what to ask for. Sometimes we need to be protected from our own prayers. Imagine the thousands of people who are praying at the same time for the one remaining parking space in downtown Chicago, Los Angeles, or New York City. If all their prayers were answered yes, there would be a colossal implosion as they all arrived at the parking space simultaneously. C. S. Lewis summed up our limitations by observing, "If God had granted all the silly prayers I've made in my life, where should I be now?"

Why aren't prayers answered always answered yes? It's a blessing in disguise that they are not.

BE CAREFUL WHAT YOU ASK FOR

In a recent Gallup poll, the top five prayer topics were family well-being, thanks, forgiveness, emotional strength, and personal peace. Still, a great many people regard prayer mainly as a way to acquire physical things.

The habit is not new, of course. Meister Eckhart, Germany's great thirteenth-century mystic, deplored this use of prayer. He lamented in his sermons that people use God like a cow, only for the milk and cheese he can give. Eckhart probably knew that the word *prayer* comes from the Latin *precarius*, "obtained by begging," and *precari*, "to entreat"—to ask earnestly, beseech, implore.

However, just because we ask for something in prayer does not necessarily mean we are being greedy. We may ask for our health to improve so we may be of greater service to others. We may request that our finances improve so we can establish a project to help persons in need. We may ask for a greater capacity for compassion and love.

Those who do pray out of greed should beware. Prayer has built-in disciplinary devices for those who abuse it. We get a hint of this in folktales about "the revenge of the Good Fairy," about which anthropologist Mary Catherine Bateson has written eloquently. These stories warn of the paradoxes and dilemmas contained in unrestrained self-ishness.

Bateson has discovered that these stories are universal. She cites the classic example of King Midas, who wanted everything he touched to turn to gold—and it did. Like some omnipotent alchemist, he went around transmuting all the things he loved into the dead, gleaming stuff. No one was safe from him, including those he loved. As a result, the man's life became a tragedy. Bateson also mentions a tale about a couple who wished for two hundred dollars and then received it as compensation for the accidental death of their son. Later they wished him back to life, only to discover that he was so deformed that they hurriedly wished him back to death again. Then there was the man who wished for a penis long enough to touch the ground—and suddenly found himself with no legs.

The fact that tales of the Good Fairy are universal suggests that they serve some valuable purpose. It has been suggested that they play a role in bringing up children. Children often ask for the most outrageous things. Sometimes their wishes are destructive, as when they wish for the death of parents or siblings. Perhaps Good Fairy tales evolved to teach them the hidden dangers of wishing unwisely.

The Good Fairy's warnings also apply to greedy prayers. I remember seeing a cartoon in *Out of Time* journal in which a man is praying, "Destroy my enemies, O God." Next: "God grant me one request: Destroy my very worst enemy." Next: A lightning bolt descends from the heavens—"ᴢᴀᴘ!"—and incinerates him. Next: The man's voice rises from his ashes, "Let me rephrase that."

This scenario is rooted in Greek mythology. When Semele, the mother of Dionysus, asked her lover Zeus to display himself in all his splendor, he obliged—destroying her with thunderbolts. As Orson Welles put it, "When the gods want to punish us, they answer our prayers." Or as writer Susan Ertz said, "Millions pray for immortality who do not know what to do with themselves on a rainy Sunday afternoon." The lesson seems to be, "Be careful what you ask for; you may get it."

I know a man who devised a type of prayer I had never before heard described. He called it "introductory prayer" because he prefaced all his prayers with it. It was a simple request in which he asked for the wisdom to know how to pray. Then one day it occurred to him that this was not quite right, either, and that he needed an introduction to his introductory prayer. So he prayed for the wisdom of knowing how to pray for the wisdom of how to pray. The first time he did so he burst out laughing, because he saw he was caught in an infinite regression: The introductions could go on forever and he would never get to the meat of his prayer. Suddenly his entire prayer enterprise seemed superfluous. He ditched *all* words—introductions as well as the prayer that followed—in favor of a prayer of silence, which he found to be the most fulfilling of all.

BEWARE OF NEGATIVE PRAYER

Most cultures, except ours, have believed that individuals can harm others with their thoughts even at a distance, even when the "recipient" is unaware of the attempt.

Many claim that "God is love" and that prayer in principle could never be used to hurt another creature. This may reflect the attempt "to keep God's skirts clean," as philosopher Alan Watts put it. But in fact, the Bible is full of hexes and curses; God's skirts may not be as clean as we think. The prophet Elisha, for example, caused forty-two children to be eaten by bears for making fun of his baldness (2 Kings 2:23–24); the apostle Paul struck a sorcerer blind (Acts 13:11); and even Jesus blasted an apparently innocent fig tree for not bearing fruit (Matthew 21:19, Mark 11:13–14, 20–22). Are these curses and not "negative prayer"? Maybe, but to the children devoured by bears, to the blinded sorcerer, and to the fig tree, it probably made little difference whether they were done in by a curse, a hex, or a negative prayer.

Some cultures have made little distinction between curses and negative prayers. An example is Polynesia, which was home to a custom called the "death prayer." This ritual spread to the Hawaiian Islands and has been studied in some detail. The Kahuna shamans used it only in dealing with individuals who were causing immense social upset and would not respond to any other measure. The shamans would gather on one island and pray to death the person on a distant island, without his or her knowledge. A nonlocal, distant curse or a negative prayer? You decide. In any event, this is not the type of hexing associated with the tradition of voodoo, in which the hexed individual is generally informed of the curse and thereafter cooperates with the dire prediction. In the death prayer, the victim *did not know.* This means the death cannot be attributed to suggestion, expectation, or negative placebo ("nocebo") effects.

Almost all cultures have taken for granted that there is a negative, shadow side to prayer, and they have devised a variety of methods to protect against these events. Elaborate rituals, counterprayers, images, amulets, and various behaviors are believed to annul the noxious effects and provide immunity. Even the Lord's Prayer says, "Deliver us from evil," which sounds suspiciously like a prayer of protection.

Most persons appear convinced that "real" prayer cannot harm. If they observe negative effects following prayer, they insist that it really wasn't the prayer's "fault." If the prayer had been genuine, the effects would not have been negative. Anything to keep God's skirts clean. But perhaps we should not dismiss the negative possibilities too quickly. If these effects are real and we hide our eyes, we may make ourselves exceedingly vulnerable.

Occasionally people believe they have caused harm to befall others as a result of their prayers, even though these people and their prayers may be loving and compassionate. One man wrote that he prayed "Thy will be done" for his sick wife, who suffered from a far-advanced brain tumor. She died. Certain that his prayers played a role in her death, he was overcome with a sense of guilt. As a result of counseling from his minister, he was able to go beyond this belief and see that her death was a compassionate outcome to a terrible situation.

Can prayer harm? Some religious folk apparently think so. When the researchers of Spindrift were conducting laboratory experiments on the effects of prayer, parishioners opposed to the studies were praying for their defeat. They felt the experiments were blasphemous, and they used prayer to sabotage them.

Consider this woman's true story:

> During the early seventies I was deeply involved in my personal development, practicing meditation and yoga, reading extensively in areas of meta-

physics and world religions. At that time a relative, an aunt by marriage, came to visit for a few days. As we visited, we seemed to share some common interests and ideas about faith, healing, prayer, and meditation.

Several weeks later, after she had returned to her home on the East Coast, I received a vitriolic letter from her. She condemned books she had seen on my shelves, saying I must burn all books on yoga, Eastern and Western religions other than traditional Christianity, all the books of a metaphysical nature. She labeled them "satanic" and "of the devil," saying they must be destroyed so that they wouldn't get into the hands of others who might read them. This was the first indication to me of our different basic perspectives on the topics we'd talked about. Instead of destroying the books, I destroyed the letter.

A few days passed, and I thought no more of the matter. Then I began to have strange "headaches" each morning right at 9:00 A.M. For a few minutes I would feel as if my brain resembled a mass of cooked spaghetti on a plate. I couldn't think straight. The feeling and image would soon pass and I'd be fine until the next day. For help in understanding what this might indicate, I turned to a friend who was a psychiatrist.

He had previously worked with me on some intensive psychotherapy followed by classes on meditation and healing. After questioning me awhile, he suggested that the next time I began to feel that way, I was to imagine a telegraph wire leading out from me to see where it went. Then to imagine that wire being flooded with love, pouring out universal love to whoever was at the other end of the wire.

I followed his instructions, and to my surprise the wire went immediately to the East Coast community where my relative lived. That really was a surprise! As I flooded that wire with universal love, the feeling of the scrambled mass of spaghetti that had begun to develop dissipated. After doing that imagery two or three days, the problem went away completely and has never returned.

After the arrival of this relative's letter, I learned that she had become deeply involved in [a particular religious movement] which was beginning to gain national attention. She had told me that daily at noon she spent a few minutes in prayer. Noon her time on the East Coast was 9:00 A.M. my time on the West Coast.

This was a strong lesson for me in the power of prayer. If her thoughts three thousand miles away could affect me that way, what other greater powers could thoughts and words have? Distance was no object. I gained an even greater respect for the power of prayer. I became even more careful about the content of my own prayers . . . and thoughts.

Not only did I learn that for myself, but over the years I've had the opportunity to lead workshops and retreats on prayer and meditation. In these, I pass on to others the importance of a healthy respect for the power of prayer. We talk about wording, imaging, and the various phrases one can include in prayer — "If it be Your will . . . ," "In keeping with the greater good for all . . . ," and other phrases.

This account illustrates some interesting points:

- Negative, harmful thoughts can come not only from individuals who are mean-spirited and evil, but also from people who are devoutly religious, as was this woman's friend. Anyone who is intolerant and narrow can be a source of harm to others. This does not mean such people are *consciously* praying for the harm of another. It is more likely, rather, that the negative thoughts originate in the *unconscious* mind and that the individuals are totally unaware they are harboring harmful attitudes about another.

• The woman whose mind was "scrambled" did not simply adopt a defensive posture and resort to prayers or rituals of protection; she responded with love. She compassionately tried to help the distant friend who felt negatively toward her. Although we do not know the effect of this strategy on the other person, we do know her own symptoms resolved, and she felt protected.

It is striking how much negativity we can give off in the name of prayer. When we pray for our team to win the Superbowl, we're praying for the defeat of another group of athletes and for the bitter disappointment of their fans. When we pray for our army to be victorious, we are indirectly asking for the suffering and death of our enemies. That does not mean we should retire into passivity and paralysis, but we should be aware of the consequences of what we ask for.

Today, most people believe prayer results in something positive or that it is neutral and does nothing at all. Almost never do we consider the possibility that prayer can be harmful. Stuck in our beliefs that prayer is either nice or neutral, we find it convenient to ignore prayer. Prayer has become a luxury, something we can drag out of our arsenal if the going gets rough. If we took seriously prayer's negative side, we would not be so sanguine, and we would respect the power of prayer much more than we do now. Knowing that prayer could harm us, we would be on our toes. Prayer would become real in every living moment, not an optional frill that can conveniently be ignored.

PRAYER HELPS US BE WARRIORS,
NOT WORRIERS

Following a naval battle between Athens and Sparta during the Peloponnesian War, many ships were sinking and hundreds of sailors were floundering in the sea. One man was praying loudly to the goddess Athena to save him, but he was obviously drowning. A shipmate, clinging to a nearby piece of wreckage, saw his plight and shouted, "Pray to Athena, but move your arms at the same time!"

We can all recognize the tendency for spiritual practice, including prayer, to spiral into inactivity. Thus the German proverb, "God gives the nuts, but he does not crack them," and the caution of Saint John Chrysostom, archbishop of Constantinople in the fourth century C.E., "Feeding the hungry is a greater work than raising the dead."

Prayer *can* be used as a substitute for action, and throughout history those who pray have often gained a reputation for being passive and avoiding the real problems of the world. The monastery and convent are constants in every religion, and there have always been individuals who have withdrawn in solitude and prayer in order to leave the misery and messiness of the world behind.

The British theologian-physicist John Polkinghorne, president of Queens' College, Cambridge, sees no conflict between prayer and action. "Prayer is not a substitute for action, but a spur to it," he observes. "If my elderly neighbour is tiresomely repetitious in the telling of the stories of his youth, I do not absolve myself from the responsibility of patiently listening yet again simply by praying for him." Along the same lines, C. S. Lewis once remarked, "I am often praying for others when I should be doing things for them. It's so much easier to pray for a bore than to go and see him."

Prayer often clarifies our vision of what needs to be done. But we should not expect to emerge from prayer wearing a celestial halo, charged for battle, like Joan of Arc following her revelations. The interplay between prayer and action is usually more subtle. More often, the understanding of one's task unfolds gradually from the sense of reverence, sacredness, and prayerfulness that starts to permeate our life as a whole, not from a highly charged moment during a specific prayer.

Psychologist Ira Progoff relates an event in the life of Abraham Lincoln that reveals these subtle yet profound connections. Lincoln had a rich prayer life and is regarded as one of our most spiritual presidents. In his early years he had intimations that meaningful work lay ahead for him but that he would have to refine his intellect and acquire professional skills if he was to fulfill his destiny. In his frontier environment, however, few tools or opportunities for professional development were available, and Lincoln feared that his hopes would never be fulfilled.

One day a stranger came by with a barrel full of odds and ends and old newspapers, and he offered to sell the lot to Lincoln for a dollar. Realizing the man was needy, Lincoln, with his characteristic kindness, gave him a dollar, although he had no idea how the barrel's contents would be of any use. When he later cleared out the barrel, he found among the junk an almost complete edition of Blackstone's *Commentaries.* These books helped Lincoln become a lawyer and eventually enter politics.

The reverence and kindness Lincoln felt for others, which are often the fruits of prayer, created an opening for a life-changing event that otherwise might not have happened. Lincoln did not get zapped during prayer with a sudden revelation of his life's work. Humble ingredients—a barrel of junk, a stranger down on his luck, a dollar, and Lincoln's innate compassion—combined unspectacularly to help shape the destiny of a nation and affect millions of lives.

"It is no good angling for the rich moments," C. S. Lewis also said, in full appreciation of experiences like Lincoln's:

> God sometimes seems to speak to us most inti-
> mately when He catches us, as it were, off our
> guard. Our preparations to receive him often have
> the opposite effect. . . . "The altar must often be
> built in one place in order that the fire from
> heaven may descend *somewhere else.*"

Our preference for the dazzling "rich moments" is one reason we leave off doing the work that needs to be done in our troubled world. We seem to be increasingly addicted to the spectacular manifestations of spiritual life—the high-octane visions, paranormal experiences, stunning revelations, miracles, and so on. Waiting for them to happen, we become insensitive to the central fact of life: It is *all* a miracle, down to the most ordinary details.

In 1987 we experienced a "Harmonic Convergence," a date prefigured in arcane prophecy that some visionaries believed would be an important event in the evolution of the human race. I neither understood nor cared much about whether the event was based on superstition or fact, but I was fascinated by the way great numbers of people were being energized psychologically as the convergence grew closer. To catch the spirit I decided to participate on the appointed morning in a sunrise gathering on an expansive grassy field on the outskirts of Dallas, where I lived at the time. I arrived with hundreds of celebrants in the predawn darkness. We groped our way along and formed a circle and held hands. Someone started singing a flower generation song, we all chimed in, and the old magic of the sixties came alive. A rosy sun gradually ascended and the shadows fell away, and we stood in silence for a long while. Joy and gratitude were palpable, and people wept. Eventually the group silently dispersed, and my heart was full.

Walking back to my car, I passed a young man in his early twenties sitting dejectedly on the hood of his auto, staring into space. He appeared disconsolate and on the brink of tears. "Are you okay?" I asked. He did not reply for a while. Finally he said, "Nothing happened. Not a damned thing. Nothing, nothing, nothing!"

Nothing happened except miracles: We were surrounded by Sun, Earth, Life, Consciousness, Love. What could be added?

Utopia comes from Greek words meaning "not in a place." If Utopia is not in "a" place, then it is in all places. And if in all places, then it is also at all times. Utopia, we come to realize, is *here* and *now*. Welcome, young man on the hood, to Utopia.

Prayer can reveal to us that waiting for a miraculous call to action is unnecessary. The call to activity will never be more miraculous than the here-and-now. We already are awash in the miraculous; there are no rich moments we need wait for. It is time to get off the hood, enter the world, and work.

The great heroes and heroines of history and legend did not wait until they had perfected themselves psychologically or until all their prayers were answered before taking action. There is no evidence that Arthur, Gawain, Beowulf, Odysseus—or St. Francis, St. John of the Cross, Hildegarde, St. Teresa, Julian of Norwich, and Florence Nightingale—were completely healthy psychologically. Indeed, there is much evidence they were not. In addition, many of them had terrible physical afflictions as well.

I cannot recall the last time I heard *guts* and *courage* and *heroism* mentioned in a lecture or a weekend seminar. Can we go from being worriers to warriors? The task is hazardous, but it has always been so. As a friend puts it, "The spiritual life is not for wimps." Many who step forward will not survive. The heroic die. But we must engage the problems we face, including our own, and not analyze or pray them to death.

Prayer *or* action? The question evaporates. We must pray and move our arms at the same time.

EPILOGUE

At a prayer meeting on board a ship bound for London in 1931, where he was traveling to plead the cause of independence for India, Mahatma Gandhi said,

> [Prayer] has saved my life. . . . I had my share of the bitterest public and private experiences. They threw me into temporary despair. If I was able to get rid of that despair it was because of prayer. . . . It came out of sheer necessity as I found myself in a plight where I could not possibly be happy without it. And as time went on my faith in God increased and more irresistible became the yearning for prayer. Life seemed to be dull and vacant without it. . . . In spite of despair staring me in the face on the political horizon, I have never lost my peace. . . . That peace comes from prayer. . . . I am indifferent as to the form. Everyone is a law unto himself in that respect. . . . Let everyone try and find that as a result of daily prayer he adds something new to his life.

Although we, like Gandhi, may come to prayer not by choice but by necessity, we often find, with time, that we can hardly do without it. Prayer nourishes us so greatly that it seems necessary for our very existence. But in our enthusiasm for prayer, let us not forget the Mahatma's ringing endorsement of tolerance, made necessary because in some sense, "Everyone is a law unto himself."

In addition to tolerance, *simplicity* is also a hallmark of authentic spiritual practice. The Dalai Lama has said, "My religion is very simple. My religion is kindness."

So, in the spirit of tolerance and simplicity, I end this book hoping the reader will set aside all the preceding comments and embark on his or her individual journey of prayer. Although this can be a solitary journey, it need not be lonely. Why should it be?—if you pray for me, and I for you. . . .

APPENDIX

GETTING ON A PRAYER LIST

If you desire the prayers of others, consider enrolling your name on a prayer list. Here's how.

THE INTERNET

If the idea of cyberspace isn't too impersonal, check the commercial computer services such as the Internet, America Online, Genie, and CompuServe. All have active religious sections; ask whether they have active prayer services.

SBCnet (the Southern Baptist Convention's network) and PresbyNet (run by the Presbyterians) have several thousand subscribers and are growing rapidly. They are almost certain to offer electronic prayer lists.

NATIONAL NEWSPAPERS

The New Times, a national newspaper, offers a prayer ministry for those who wish to use it. If you want its reader community to pray for you, simply send in your initials (not your name and not the reason you desire prayer; the service is anonymous). Initials are published for a month; if you want to be prayed for longer, send

in your initials again. The service is free, although dona-
tions are accepted to cover costs. Address:

> *The New Times*
> P. O. Box 51186
> Seattle, WA 98115–1186

ECUMENICAL PRAYER SERVICES

If electronic prayer and newspaper communities don't
appeal to you, you may prefer to contact one of the following ecumenical prayer services.

This list was assembled by Vivian Berg of Marina del
Rey, California. Most of the prayer groups listed are in
California—presumably not because Californians need
more prayer than the rest of us, but because Mrs. Berg is a
Californian and knows more about the prayer activity in
her own area than elsewhere. Mrs. Berg is interested in
expanding the list to include all the ecumenical prayer
groups in the United States. As far as I can determine,
such a comprehensive listing currently does not exist.
Please send any information about prayer groups you may
have to the following address:

Vivian Berg
14021 Marquesas Way, #307C
Marina del Rey, CA 90292

California

Discalced Carmelites
Carmel of St. Teresa
215 E. Alhambra Road
Alhambra, CA 91801
818–282–2387

Insight for Living
P.O. Box 69000
Anaheim, CA 92817
800–772–8888 (main number)
714–575–5000 (counseling number)

The Free Catholic Church
P.O. Box 1439
La Jolla, CA 92038
619–459–4275
619–459–4277 (fax)

New Thought Center of Los Angeles
1122 S. La Cienega Blvd., Suite 111
Los Angeles, CA 90035
310–652–2080
310–652–2946 (fax)

Islamic Center of Southern California
934 South Vermont Avenue
Los Angeles, CA 90020
213–382–9200

Johrei Fellowship
3068 San Marino Street
Los Angeles, CA 90020
213–387–8366

Johrei Fellowship
National Headquarters
1971 West 190th Street, Suite 280
Torrence, CA
310–523–3840
310–523–3843

Self-Realization Fellowship
3883 San Rafael Avenue
Los Angeles, CA 90065
213–225–2471

Dominican Nuns of the Order of Preachers
The Monastery of the Angels
1977 Carmen Avenue
Los Angeles, CA 90068
213–466–2186

Ananda
14618 Tyler Foote Road
Nevada City, CA 95959
916–292–3506 (prayer group)
916–292–4100 (main number)

Unity Church, Worldwide
P.O. Box 1709
Palm Desert, CA 92261–9989

Calvary Chapel
Prayer Request Secretary (for written requests)
3800 Fairview Road
Santa Ana, CA 92704
714–979–4422 (only at night from 10 P.M. to 8 A.M.)

Jewish Healing Center
141 Alton Avenue
San Francisco, CA 94116
415–387–4999

Franciscan Poor Clare Nuns
215 E. Los Olivos Street
Santa Barbara, CA 93105
805-682-7670

Aiko Hormann Ministries
P.O. Box 926
Santa Monica, CA 90406
818-909-0959

Carmel of St. Joseph
P. O. Box 379
Solvang, CA 93464
805-686-4292

First Lutheran Church of Venice
815 Venice Blvd.
Venice, CA 90291
310-397-1230

Florida

Christian Healing Ministries, Inc.
438 West 67th Street
Jacksonville, FL 32208
904-765-3332

Coral Ridge Baptist Church
P.O. Box 16502
Jacksonville, FL 32246
904–642–2726

Illinois

National Spiritual Assembly of the Baha'i Faith
of the United States
536 Sheridan Road
Wilmette, IL 60091

Kansas

Unity Church of Overland Park
977 Antioch
Overland Park, KS 66212
913–649–3214

Maryland

New Life Clinic
Mt. Washington United Methodist Church
5800 Cottonworth Avenue
Baltimore, MD
410–561–0428

Fourth Presbyterian Church
5500 River Road
Bethesda, MD 20892
301–320–3672

Life in Jesus Community
P.O. Box 40
Libertytown, MD 21762
301–829–1577

Massachusetts

St. Joseph's Abbey
N. Spencer Road
Spencer, MA 01562
508–885–4760

Minnesota

Billy Graham Evengelistic Association
P.O. Box 779
Minneapolis, MN 55440-0779
612–338–0500

Missouri

Silent Unity
Unity Village, MO 64065–0001
800–669–7729 (free call)
816–251–3544 (Spanish-speaking)
816–246–5400
816–524–3550 (general number, Unity Village)

New York

Guideposts Magazine
39 Seminary Hill Road
Carmel, NY 10512
800–204–3772

House of Peace
1291 Allerton Avenue
Bronx, NY 10469
718–547–3230

National Center for Jewish Healing
9 East 69th Street
New York, NY 10021
212–772–6601

North Carolina

The Ecumenical Institute of Wake Forest University
and Belmont Abbey College
100 Belmont-Mount Holly Road
Belmont, NC 20802-2795
704–825–6700

Hickory Grove United Methodist Church
6401 Hickory Grove Road
Charlotte, NC 28215
704–537–4686

Church of Concord
P.O. Box 103
Concord, NC 28025
800–315–7729

International Prayer Fellowship
Box 1236
Lake Junaluska, NC 28745
704–456–4454

South Carolina

Cathedral of Love Church
5525 Highway 187
Anderson, SC 29625

Virginia

Shepherd's Heart
10875 Main Street
Suite 102
Fairfax, VA 22032
703–385–4833

Association for Research and Enlightenment, Inc.
67th Street and Atlantic Avenue
P. O. Box 595
Virginia Beach, VA 23451
804–428–3588

Christian Broadcasting Network Center/700 Club
977 Centerville Turnpike
Virginia Beach, VA 23463
804–420–0700

General

Prayer Chain (of the Lutheran Church)
213–397–1230 (main number)

———————

Science of Mind World Ministry of Prayer
213–385–0209
800–421–9600 (free call)

Most large Protestant and Catholic congregations have prayer ministries. Almost all Conservative or Orthodox synagogues will pray for those requesting prayer on Mondays, Thursdays, and Saturdays. Lay prayer lists are also common. To find them, keep your ears open; ask friends. In the unlikely event you cannot locate a prayer group, start one.

You can also join a prayer group as an intercessor—one who prays for others. This is a unique form of volunteerism. People who serve in this capacity often find that their lives become more joyful and fulfilling—evidence that prayer is good not just for the recipient but for the pray-er as well.

NOTES

AUTHOR'S NOTE

xiv "Of God himself can no man think." *The Cloud of Unknowing,*
trans. Clifton Wolters (Baltimore: Penguin Books, 1961), 59.

xiv "Whoever perceives something in God . . ." *Meister Eckhart,*
trans. Edmund Colledge and Bernard McGinn (New York:
Paulist Press, 1981), 204–5.

xiv "It is God's nature to be without a nature." *Meister Eckhart,*
trans. Raymond B. Blakney (New York: Harper & Row, 1941),
243.

INTRODUCTION

1–2 For the *Wall Street Journal* discussion of scientific studies of
prayer, see Joseph Pereira, "The Healing Power of Prayer Is
Tested by Science," *Wall Street Journal,* December 20, 1995.

2 "Recent surveys show that 75 percent of patients believe . . ."
See David B. Larson and Mary A. Greenwold Milano, "Are
Religion and Spirituality Relevant in Health Care?"
Mind/Body Medicine 1, no. 3 (1995): 147–57.

2 ". . . the majority of us actually pray for our patients." See
J. Martin and C. Carlson, "Spiritual Dimensions of Health
Psychology," in *Behavioral Therapy and Religion,* ed. W. R.
Miller and J. Martin (Beverly Hills: Sage Publications, 1988),
57–110.

2 "Statistically, God is good for you. . . ." David B. Larson, quoted
by John Boudreau, "Scientists Examine the Healing Powers of
Prayer," *Contra Costa [California] Times,* January 21, 1996.

3 ". . . a scientific paper in which prayer was tested in a modern
hospital in a large group of heart patients." The paper was

Randolph C. Byrd, "Positive Therapeutic Effects of Intercessory Prayer in a Coronary Care Unit Population," *Southern
Medical Journal* 81, no. 7 (July 1988): 826–29.

5 "Prayerlike thoughts, offered from a distance, have been
demonstrated to increase the healing rate of surgical wounds
. . ." See the research of Daniel P. Wirth, "The Effect of Non-
contact Therapeutic Touch on the Healing Rate of Full Thickness Dermal Wounds," *Subtle Energies* 1, no. 1 (1990): 1–20;
and Daniel P. Wirth, "Full Thickness Dermal Wounds Treated
with Non-contact Therapeutic Touch: A Replication and Ex-
tension," *Complementary Therapies in Medicine* 1 (1993): 127–32.

5 ". . . religious faith is associated with faster recovery from
surgery." See the research of P. Pressman, J. S. Lyons, D. B.
Larson, and J. S. Strain, "Religious Belief, Depression, and
Ambulation Status in Elderly Women with Broken Hips,"
American Journal of Psychiatry 147 (1990): 758–60; and T. E.
Oxman, D. H. Freeman, and E. D. Manheimer, "Lack of
Social Participation or Religious Strength or Comfort as Risk
Factors for Death after Cardiac Surgery in the Elderly," *Psy-
chosomatic Medicine* 57 (1995): 5–15.

PART ONE: THE EVIDENCE

9 ". . . evidence suggests that prayer, like drugs, can have effects
that can be positive, neutral, or negative." See Larry Dossey,
"When Prayer Hurts," *Healing Words: The Power of Prayer and
the Practice of Medicine* (San Francisco: HarperSanFrancisco,
1993), 145–58.

15–17   "We are not setting a trap to catch God in . . ." Deborah Rose, "Letters to the Editor," *Home Catacomb* 8, no. 8 (September 1994), 3–4. Subsequent comments by Rose also refer to this source.

20   "We need a religious system with science at its very core . . ." Margaret Mead, quoted in "Five Who Care," *Look*, April 21, 1970.

21   *"Examiner: What is electricity? . . ."* John D. Barrow, *The World Within the World* (New York: Oxford Univ. Press, 1988), 193.

22   "We shall not expect the natural sciences to give us direct insight . . ." Erwin Schrödinger, "The Spirit of Science," in *Spirit and Nature*, papers from the *Eranos Yearbooks*, ed. Joseph Campbell, Bollingen Series 30–31 (Princeton: Princeton Univ. Press, 1954), 324–25.

23   "There can never be any real opposition between religion and science . . ." Max Planck, *Where Is Science Going?* (1933; reprint, Woodbridge, CT: Ox Bow Press, 1981), 168–69.

23   "The list of great physicists who took similar views is very long. . . ." For the compiling of such views, see Ken Wilber, *Quantum Questions: The Mystical Writings of the World's Great Physicists* (Boston: Shambhala, 1984).

27   ". . . distant or intercessory prayer succeeds *without the knowledge* of the recipient." See Larry Dossey, "Prayer and Healing: Reviewing the Research," *Healing Words: The Power of Prayer and the Practice of Medicine* (San Francisco: HarperSanFrancisco, 1993), 169–96. See also Daniel J. Benor, *Healing Research* (Munich: Helix Verlag, 1993). Address: Windeckstrasse 82, D–81375 Munich, Germany.

29 "In a study by cardiologist Randolph Byrd involving 393 patients in the coronary care unit of San Francisco General Hospital . . ." See Randolph C. Byrd, "Positive Therapeutic Effects of Intercessory Prayer in a Coronary Care Unit Population," *Southern Medical Journal* 81, no. 7 (July 1988): 826–29.

30 "Other studies have compared the ability of people to influence the growth rates of organisms at close range . . ." See the research of J. Barry, "General and Comparative Study of the Psychokinetic Effect on a Fungus Culture," *Journal of Parapsychology* 32 (1968): 237–43; and W. Tedder and M. Monty, "Exploration of Long-distance PK: A Conceptual Replication of the Influence on a Biological System," *Research in Parapsychology* 1980 (1981): 90–93.

32 "Nobel physicist Brian Josephson of Cambridge University's Cavendish Laboratory suggests that these nonlocal *quantum* phenomena may underlie many *human* events . . ." See B. D. Josephson and F. Pallikara-Viras, "Biological Utilization of Quantum Nonlocality," *Foundations of Physics* 21 (1993): 197–207.

PART TWO: THE CONTROVERSY

37 "Each year, almost two million individuals who enter hospitals in this country acquire infections . . ." For discussion of iatrogenic illness, see Jeffrey A. Fisher, *The Plague Makers* (New York: Simon & Schuster, 1994), 31.

38 The *Physicians' Desk Reference* . . . is the medical profession's guide to prescription drugs . . ." *Physicians' Desk Reference*,

49th ed. (Montvale, NJ: Medical Economics Data Production Company, 1995).

39 "Surveys have repeatedly shown that people who opt for alternative therapies are generally *more* educated . . ." See David J. Hufford, "Cultural and Social Perspectives on Alternative Medicine: Background and Assumptions," *Alternative Therapies* 1, no. 1 (1995): 53–61; B. R. Cassileth, E. J. Lusk, T. B. Strouse, F. J. Bodenheimer, "Contemporary Unorthodox Treatments in Cancer Medicine: A Study of Patients, Treatments, and Practitioners," *Annals of Internal Medicine* 10 (1984): 105–12.

49 "More than 130 controlled laboratory studies show that prayer . . . can bring about healthful changes . . ." See Larry Dossey, "Prayer and Healing: Reviewing the Research," *Healing Words: The Power of Prayer and the Practice of Medicine* (San Francisco: HarperSanFrancisco, 1993), 169–96. See also Daniel J. Benor, *Healing Research* 1–2 (Munich: Helix Verlag, 1993). Address: Windeckstrasse 82, D–81375 Munich, Germany.

50 "Those who derive at least some strength and comfort— hope!—from religion are more likely to survive . . ." For the role of hope in healing, see "Faith Heals," *Mental Medicine Update* 4, no. 2 (1995): 1.

50 "Numerous studies in humans show that we can die as a result of dire beliefs . . ." For a discussion of death resulting from hopelessness, see Larry Dossey, *Meaning & Medicine* (New York: Bantam, 1993).

56 "Complicating this area is the considerable evidence that prayer can harm as well as heal. . . ." See Larry Dossey, "When

Notes

Notes

Prayer Hurts," in *Healing Words* (San Francisco: HarperSan-Franciso, 199), 145–58.

56 "Dr. Anthony Rippo, internist and founder of the Santa Fe Institute of Medicine and Prayer . . ." The Santa Fe Institute for Medicine and Prayer may be contacted at 906 Canyon Road, Santa Fe, NM 87501.

57–58 "Several years ago my friend's husband, Stephen, was involved in a near-fatal auto accident . . ." Personal communication to the author, June 20, 1995. Used with permission.

62 "If I knew my doctor was praying for me, I'd get another doctor." Annie L. Gaylor, quoted by Steve Brewer, "UNM [University of New Mexico] Study on Prayer Raises Ire," *Albuquerque Journal*, May 3, 1995.

65 "In May 1995 . . ." See Charles Marwick, "Should Physicians Prescribe Prayer for Health? Spiritual Aspects of Well-Being Considered," *Journal of the American Medical Association* 273, no. 20 (May 24, 1995): 1561–62.

66 "Today over 130 controlled scientific studies investigating the effects of intercessory prayer have been carried out . . ." For discussion of these studies, see Larry Dossey, *Healing Words: The Power of Prayer and the Practice of Medicine* (San Francisco: HarperSanFrancisco, 1993); see also Daniel J. Benor, *Healing Research* 1–2 (Munich: Helix Verlag, 1993). For discussion of the 250 studies on religious practice and health, see Jeffrey S. Levin, "Religion and Health: Is There an Association, Is It Valid and Is It Causal?" *Social Science and Medicine*

38 (1994): 1475–1482. Also see J. S. Levin and P. L. Schiller, "Is There a Religious Factor in Health?" *Journal of Religion and Health* 267 (1987): 9–36. See also the pioneering work of David B. Larson, M.D. Particularly recommended is his review, with Susan S. Larson, of the religion-and-health field, *The Forgotten Factor in Physical and Mental Health: What Does the Research Show?* This information is available in the form of a self-directed teaching module and can be obtained from the National Institute for Healthcare Research (David B. Larson, M.D., president), 6110 Executive Blvd., Suite 680, Rockville, MD 20852.

68 "If my doctor prayed for my recovery, I'd consider a malpractice lawsuit." Richard J. Goss, quoted by Joseph Pereira, "The Healing Power of Prayer Is Tested by Science," *Wall Street Journal*, December 20, 1995.

69 "In one survey, more than 75 percent of patients believed that their physician should address spiritual issues as part of their medical care. . . ." David B. Larson and Mary A. Greenwold Milano, "Are Religion and Spirituality Clinically Relevant?" *Mind/Body Medicine* 1, no. 3 (1995): 147–57. For doctor-patient discussions of religious issues, see T. A. Maugans and W. C. Wadland, "Religion and Family Medicine: A Survey of Physicians and Patients," *Journal of Family Practice* 31 (1991): 210–13. For the attitudes of hospital patients toward their doctor's use of prayer, see D. E. King and B. Bushwick, "Beliefs and Attitudes of Hospital Inpatients about Faith Healing and Prayer," *Journal of Family Practice* 39 (1994): 349–52.

PART THREE: WHAT IS PRAYER?

77 Plutarch quoted in C. L. Sulzberger, *Go Gentle into the Good Night* (Englewood Cliffs, NJ: Prentice-Hall, 1976), 24.

78 "When put to the test . . ." For discussion of scientific experiments in nonlocal prayer, see Larry Dossey, *Healing Words: The Power of Prayer and the Practice of Medicine* (San Francisco: HarperSanFrancisco, 1993).

79 "These cases are unexplainable . . ." For the capacity of consciousness to function at a distance, see Rupert Sheldrake, *Seven Experiments That Could Change the World* (New York: Riverhead, 1995), 33–72.

92 "Many experiments in prayer have been done in the past three decades, involving people from various religious persuasions." For results of these studies, see Deborah Rose, "The Spindrift Story," *Home Catacomb* 9, no. 8 (1995): 8.

93 "Is a Mercedes Benz and a well-stocked portfolio a sign of God's grace?" From "Notes on the Catacomb Wall," *Home Catacomb* 9, no. 2 (1995): 11.

93 "You can actually tell God what you would like his part in the covenant to be! . . ." Television evangelist Robert Tilton, quoted by Richard N. Ostling, "Heresy on the Airwaves," *Time*, March 5, 1990, 62.

94 "God pulls a man out of the cosmic cooker . . ." *Stray Light Times*, no. 1 (January 13, 1993): 2.

94–95 "To acquire the knack of getting his petitions answered . . ." Aldous Huxley, *The Perennial Philosophy* (New York: Harper & Row, 1944), 220–21.

95　"The just man loves God for nothing." Meister Eckhart,
quoted in Raymond B. Blakney, *Meister Eckhart* (New York:
Harper & Row, 1941), 241.

96–97　"There was a seventeen-year-old boy who had been in a disas-
trous motorcycle accident. . . ." Betsy MacGregor, "Health
Reform and the Sacred," a group discussion, *Advances* 11, no. 1
(Winter 1995): 37–54.

97–98　"I asked God for strength . . ." "Prayer of an Unknown Confederate Soldier," *The Oxford Book of Prayer* (New York: Oxford
Univ. Press, 1985), 119.

98　"It is only possible to live happily ever after . . ." Margaret
Bonnano, "Sunbeams," *The Sun*, no. 198 (May 1992): 40.

99　"And some, like me, are just beginning to guess . . ." Adair
Lara, quoted in "Sunbeams," *The Sun*, no. 222 (June 1994): 40.

PART FOUR: HOW TO PRAY

104　"When their scores were analyzed separately . . ." E. Haraldsson
and T. Thorsteinsson, "Psychokinetic Effects on Yeast: An Ex-
ploratory Experiment," *Research in Parapsychology* (Metuchen,
NJ: Scarecrow Press, 1973), 20–21.

104　"In these tests, as in the Iceland experiment, the more experi-
enced practitioners produced the more powerful outcomes."
For discussion of this research, see Spindrift, *The Spindrift Pa-
pers: Exploring Prayer and Healing Through the Experimental
Test* (Lansdale, PA: Spindrift, 1994). See also Larry Dossey,
"The Spindrift Experiments," *Recovering the Soul* (New York:
Bantam, 1989), 58–62.

108 "There was a child went forth every day . . ." Walt Whitman, "There Was a Child Went Forth," *A Choice of Whitman's Verse* (London: Faber and Faber, 1968), 21.

112 "The evidence supporting these widespread effects is abundant . . ." For a review of these studies, see Daniel J. Benor, *Healing Research*, vols. 1–2 (Munich: Helix Verlag, 1993); and Larry Dossey, *Healing Words: The Power of Prayer and the Practice of Medicine* (San Francisco: HarperSanFrancisco, 1993).

112 "Researchers have begun to study the health benefits of having pets." Research by Dr. Aaron H. Katcher, Prof. Ann Ottney Cain, Dr. Herbert Benson, Peter R. Messent, and Sharon L. Smith is discussed in Joan Arehart-Treichel, "Pets: The Health Benefits," *Science News* 121 (1982): 220–23.

115 "And pets, like prayer, save lives." Dr. Erika Friedmann's research is discussed by Bruce Bower, "Stress Goes to the Dogs," *Science News* 140 (1991): 285.

118–22 Personal communication from Hilary Petit, D.V.M., Sacramento, California, April 1995. Used with permission.

124 "Many a Christian prays faintly . . ." C. S. Lewis, *Letters to Malcolm: Chiefly on Prayer* (New York: Harcourt Brace Jovanovich, 1964), 114.

126 "I throw myself down in my chamber . . ." John Donne, quoted in "Sunbeams," *The Sun*, no. 228 (December 1994): 40.

127 "Does God have a set way of prayer . . ." Dorothy Day, quoted in "Sunbeams," *The Sun*, no. 233 (March 1995): 40.

134 "As Richard Foster said, Francis 'seemed not so much a man praying . . . ' " Richard J. Foster, *Prayer: Finding the Heart's True Home* (San Francisco: HarperSanFrancisco, 1992), 117.

136 "It isn't morally superior to use one method [of prayer] over another. . . ." Deborah Rose, "The Spindrift Story," *Home Catacomb* 9, no. 8 (November 1995): 7.

136 "People ask, What type of prayer should I say? . . ." Deborah Rose, "The Spindrift Story," *Home Catacomb* 9, no. 2 (March 1995): 11–16.

138–39 "The kingdom of heaven is within . . ." Michael Toms, *Interviews with Joseph Campbell* (audiocassette series). New Dimensions Radio, 475 Gate Five Road, Suite 206, Sausalito, CA 94966.

139 "According to legend, the gods were arguing over where to hide the secret of life . . ." This tale is recounted by James W. Jones, *In the Middle of This Road We Call Our Life* (San Francisco: HarperSanFrancisco, 1994), 24–25.

145 "I believe that divine and human coherence in prayer . . ." John Polkinghorne, "Can a Scientist Pray?" *Explorations in Science and Theology*, Templeton London Lectures at the RSA (London: The Royal Society for the Encouragement of Arts, Manufactures & Commerce, 1993), 17–22.

150–51 "In December 1992 I was diagnosed with an aggressive cancer of the urinary bladder . . ." Abridged account of personal communication, 1995. Used with permission.

151–53 "Within two years, my husband and I had lost our jobs. . . ." Abridged account of personal communication, 1995. Used with permission.

153 "Throughout human history, dreams and night prayers have served the great priests . . ." Night prayers are making a comeback. See Phil Cousineau's *Prayers At 3 A.M.: Poems, Songs,*

Chants, and Prayers for the Middle of the Night (San Francisco: HarperSanFrancisco, 1995).

158–59 "Mysticism can have serious health threats. . . ." Karen Armstrong, *Visions of God* (New York: Bantam, 1994), x–xi, 5.

161 "Deborah Rose . . . gives the analogy of praying for healthy tomato plants." See Deborah Rose, "The Spindrift Story," *Home Catacomb* 9, no. 2 (March 1995): 11–16. Rose's comments on the "ordering force" in prayer are also from this source.

164 "In my kitchen at home we did not really need the milk to stay fresh . . ." Deborah Rose, "The Spindrift Story," *Home Catacomb* 9, no. 9 (December 1995): 9.

166–73 The section "Praying for Corn in Iowa" is compiled from the following sources: Joyce Vogelman, "Power of Prayer: Congregations Pray for Thousands of Iowa Farmers During Harvest," *Iowa Farmer*, September 30, 1995; Jean Caspers-Simmet, "Help from High Places? Pastor Inspired Parishioners to Pray at Harvest," *Agri News* 40, no. 22 (November 23, 1995); and personal written communication from the Reverend Karl E. Goodfellow, December 1995.

170 "Know our surroundings . . ." Reverend Mary K. Green, devotional for October 10, *God's Harvest—God's People*, ed. Karl E. Goodfellow (Guttenberg, IA: United Methodist Church, 1996), 5.

170–71 "Accidents happen so quickly. . . ." Liz Goodfellow, *God's Harvest—God's People*, ed. Karl E. Goodfellow (Guttenberg, IA: United Methodist Church, 1996), 23.

173 "The Reverend Goodfellow has been swamped with requests . . ." Interested individuals may contact the Reverend Doctor Karl E. Goodfellow at P. O. Box 706, Guttenberg, IA 52052.

175 "If God had granted all the silly prayers I've made . . ." C. S. Lewis, *Letters to Malcolm: Chiefly on Prayer* (New York: Harcourt Brace Jovanovich, 1964), 28.

176 "We get a hint of this in folktales about 'the revenge of the Good Fairy,' . . ." See Mary Catherine Bateson's research on this folktale theme in her article "The Revenge of the Good Fairy," *Whole Earth Review*, no. 55 (Summer 1987): 34–48.

178 "In a four-panel cartoon strip . . ." From *Out of Time* (a journal of Endeavor Academy), Lake Delton, WI: Academy Publishing (first quarter 1993), 5.

180 "Some cultures have made little distinction between curses and negative prayers . . ." See Larry Dossey, "When Prayer Hurts," *Healing Words: The Power of Prayer and the Practice of Medicine* (San Francisco: HarperSanFrancisco, 1993), 145–58.

182 "Can prayer harm? Some religious folk apparently think so. . . ." For one example of religious folk opposed to prayer studies, see Theodore Rockwell, "The Bridge of Sighs: Problems of Building a Sci/Psi Bridge," *Home Catacomb* 8, no. 9 (October 1994): 1–3.

182–85 "During the early seventies I was deeply involved in my personal development . . ." Personal communication with the author, June 20, 1995. Used with permission.

188 "God gives the nuts, but he does not crack them." Quoted in *Sunbeams: A Book of Quotations*, ed. Sy Safransky (Berkeley: North Atlantic Books, 1990), 14.

188 "Feeding the hungry is a greater work . . ." Quoted in "Sunbeams," *The Sun*, no. 237 (September 1995): 40.

189 "Prayer is not a substitute for action . . ." John Polkinghorne, "Can a Scientist Pray?" *Explorations in Science and Theology*, Templeton London Lectures at the RSA (London: Royal Society for the Encouragement of Arts, Manufactures & Commerce, 1993), 17–22.

189 "I am often praying for others when I should be doing things for them. . . ." C. S. Lewis, *Letters to Malcolm: Chiefly on Prayer* (New York: Harcourt Brace Jovanovich, 1964), 66.

189 "Psychologist Ira Progoff relates an event in the life of Abraham Lincoln . . ." See Ira Progoff, *Jung, Synchronicity, and Human Destiny* (New York: Julian Press, 1973), 170–71.

191 "It is no good angling for the rich moments . . ." C. S. Lewis, *Letters to Malcolm: Chiefly on Prayer* (New York: Harcourt Brace Jovanovich, 1964), 117.

EPILOGUE

197 "[Prayer] has saved my life . . ." Mahatma Gandhi, cited in Louis Fischer, ed., *The Essential Gandhi* (New York: Random House, 1962), 309–10.

FURTHER READINGS

BOOKS AND TAPES BY LARRY DOSSEY, M.D.

Healing Words: The Power of Prayer and the Practice of Medicine. San Francisco: HarperSanFrancisco, 1993

Meaning & Medicine. New York: Bantam, 1991.

Recovering the Soul. New York: Bantam, 1989.

Beyond Illness. Boston: Shambhala, 1984.

Space, Time & Medicine. Boston: Shambhala, 1982.

The Power of Prayer: Connecting with the Power of the Universe. Six audiocassettes. Nightingale Conant, 7300 North Lehigh Avenue, Niles, IL 60714, 800–572–2770.

How to Have a Miracle: Dynamics of Healing. Institute of Noetic Sciences 1993 "Heart of Healing" Conference. Video and audiocassette available. Institute of Noetic Sciences, 475 Gate Five Road, Suite 300, Sausalito, CA 94966.

Recovering the Soul: A Scientific and Spiritual Search. Video and audiocassette. Mystic Fire Video, 523 Broadway, Suite 604, New York, NY 10012.

Alternative Therapies in Health and Medicine. Dr. Dossey is executive editor of this new journal in the field of complementary/alternative medicine. Each issue contains an editorial by Dr. Dossey. *Alternative Therapies*, P.O. Box 611, Holmes, PA 19043, 800–345–8112.

PRAYER AND MEDITATION

Appleton, George, ed. *The Oxford Book of Prayer.* New York: Oxford University Press, 1987.

Armstrong, Karen. *Visions of God.* New York: Bantam, 1994.

Benson, Herbert. *Your Maximum Mind.* New York: Times Books, 1987.

———. *Beyond the Relaxation Response.* New York: Times Books, 1984.

———. *The Relaxation Response*. New York: Morrow: 1975.

Benson, Herbert, and Eileen M. Stuart. *The Wellness Book*. New York: Birch Lane Press, 1992.

Bloch, Douglas. *I Am with You Always*. New York: Bantam, 1992.

———. *Words That Heal*. New York: Bantam, 1988.

Cahill, Thomas. *Jesus' Little Instruction Book*. New York: Bantam, 1994.

Campbell, Camille. *Meditations with John of the Cross*. Santa Fe: Bear, 1989.

———. *Meditations with Teresa of Avila*. Santa Fe: Bear, 1985.

Castelli, Jim, ed. *How I Pray: People of Different Religions Share with Us That Most Sacred and Intimate Act of Faith*. New York: Ballantine, 1994.

Caulfield, Sean. *The Experience of Praying*. New York: Paulist Press, 1980.

Cousineau, Phil, ed. *Prayers at 3 A.M.: Poems, Songs, Chants, and Prayers for the Middle of the Night*. San Francisco: HarperSanFrancisco, 1995.

Douglas-Klotz, Neil. *Prayers of the Cosmos: Meditations on the Aramaic Words of Jesus.*San Francisco: HarperSanFrancisco, 1990.

Gallagher, Blanche. *Meditations with Teilhard de Chardin*. Santa Fe: Bear, 1988.

Gill, Jean. *Pray As You Can: Discovering Your Own Prayer Ways*. Notre Dame, IL: Ave Maria Press, 1989.

Goleman, Daniel. *The Meditative Mind*. Los Angeles: Tarcher, 1988.

Hanh, Thich Nhat. *A Guide to Walking Meditation*. New York: Fellowship Publications, 1985.

——. *The Miracle of Mindfulness: A Manual on Meditation.* Boston: Beacon, 1976.

——. *Peace in Every Step: The Path of Mindfulness in Everyday Life.* New York: Bantam, 1976.

Kabat-Zinn, Jon. *Full Catastrophe Living: Using the Wisdom of Your Body and Mind to Face Stress, Pain and Illness.* New York: Delacorte Press, 1990.

Kaplan, Aryeh. *Jewish Meditation: A Practical Guide.* New York: Schocken, 1985.

Keating, Thomas. *Open Mind, Open Heart: The Contemplative Dimension of the Gospel.* New York: Amity House, 1986.

LeShan, Lawrence. *How to Meditate.* New York: Bantam, 1974.

Leunig, Michael. *A Common Prayer.* Collins Dove, 1990.

Levy, Joel. *Relaxation, Concentration and Meditation: Ancient Skills for Modern Minds.* London: Wisdom, 1987.

Lewis, C. S. *Letters to Malcolm: Chiefly on Prayer.* New York: Harcourt Brace Jovanovich, 1964.

Master Meditations: A Spiritual Daybook. Santa Monica, CA: IBS Press, 1990.

Michael, Chester P., and Marie C. Norissey. *Prayer and Temperament: Different Prayer Forms for Different Personality Types.* Charlottesville, VA: The Open Door, 1984.

Moore, Thomas. *Meditations.* New York: HarperCollins, 1994.

——. *Care of the Soul.* New York: HarperCollins, 1992.

Nachman, Rabbi. *Restore My Soul.* Jerusalem: Reslov Research Institute, 1980.

Paramananda, Swami. *Book of Daily Thoughts and Prayer.* Cohasset, MA: Vedanta Centre Publishers, 1977.

Prabhavananda, Swami, and Christopher Isherwood, translation and commentary. *How to Know God: The Yoga Aphorisms of Patanjali.* New York: New American Library, 1953.

Roberts, Elizabeth, and Elias Amidon. *Life Prayers.* San Francisco: HarperSanFrancisco, 1996.

——. *Earth Prayers from Around the World.* San Francisco: HarperSanFrancisco, 1991.

Rossman, Martin. *Healing Yourself.* New York: Walker, 1987; New York: Pocket Books, 1990

Singer, June. *A Gnostic Book of Hours.* San Francisco: HarperSanFrancisco, 1992.

Sponheim, Paul R., ed. *A Primer on Prayer.* Philadelphia: Fortress Press, 1988.

Steindl-Rast, Brother David. *Gratefulness, The Heart of Prayer.* New York: Paulist Press, 1984.

Uhlein, Gabrielle. *Meditations with Hildegard of Bingen.* Santa Fe: Bear, 1983.

Ulanov, Ann, and Barry Ulanov. *Primary Speech: A Psychology of Prayer.* Atlanta: John Knox Press, 1982.

Weil, Simone. *Waiting for God.* New York: Harper & Row, 1973.

Weston, Walter. *PrayWell.* Wadsworth, OH: Transitions Press, 1994.

SCIENTIFIC REFERENCES
ON PRAYER AND HEALING

Dr. Dossey's 1993 book *Healing Words,* mentioned above, contains almost all of the scientific references for experiments in prayer-based or spiritual healing.

In addition, many scientific references can be found in the Notes section of this book.

The next six references are particularly recommended:

Benor, Daniel J. *Healing Research*, Vols 1–2. Munich: Helix Verlag, 1993. Benor's books will soon be available in the United States. A landmark contribution.

Larson, David B. *The Faith Factor—Volume Two: An Annotated Bibliography of Systematic Reviews and Clinical Research on Spiritual Subjects*. National Institute for Healthcare Research, 6110 Executive Blvd., Suite 680, Rockville, MD 20952, 1995.

Larson, David B., and Susan S. Larson. *The Forgotten Factor in Physical and Mental Health: What Does the Research Show? An Independent Study Seminar*. National Institute for Healthcare Research, 6110 Executive Blvd., Suite 680, Rockville, MD 20952, 1995.

Levin, Jeffrey S., ed. *Religion in Aging and Health*. Thousand Oaks, CA: Sage, 1994.

Matthews, Dale, David B. Larson, and Constance Barry. *The Faith Factor: An Annotated Bibliography of Clinical Research on Spiritual Subjects*. National Institute for Healthcare Research, 6110 Executive Blvd., Suite 680, Rockville, MD 20952, 1995.

Murphy, Michael. *The Future of the Body*. Los Angeles: Tarcher, 1992. This encyclopedic work contains hundreds of scientific references. It deals with "what is humanly possible" and contains valuable insights into prayer and healing.

SPIRITUAL HEALING—ADDITIONAL INFORMATION

Eddy, Mary Baker. *Science and Health with Key to the Scriptures*. Boston: First Church of Christ, Scientist, 1934.

Holmes, Ernest. *The Anatomy of Healing Prayer*. The Ernest Holmes Papers, vols. 1 and 2. Compiled by George P. Bendall. Marina del Rey, CA: DeVorss, 1991.

The Home Catacomb. The school newspaper of the Grayhaven School of Christian Science Nursing. Grayhaven School of Christian Science Nursing, P.O. Box 2364, Cape May, NJ 08204.

Kelsey, Morton T. *Psychology, Medicine & Christian Healing.* San Francisco: Harper & Row, 1966.

Kunz, Dora, ed. *Spiritual Aspects of the Healing Arts.* Wheaton, IL: Quest, 1985.

Laskow, Leonard. *Healing with Love.* San Francisco: HarperSanFrancisco, 1992.

LeShan, Lawrence. *The Medium, the Mystic, and the Physicist.* New York: Viking, 1966.

Markides, Kyriacos. *Riding with the Lion: In Search of Mystical Christianity.* New York: Viking Penguin, 1994. This is one of a series of fascinating books by Markides dealing with Daskalos, a Cypriot healer in the Greek Orthodox tradition.

McCall, Father Peter, and Maryanne Lacy. *Rise and Be Healed.* Bronx, NY: House of Peace, 1992.

———. *An Invitation to Healing.* Bronx, NY: House of Peace, 1985.

Peel, Robert. *Spiritual Healing in a Scientific Age.* San Francisco: Harper & Row, 1987.

Puryear, Meredith Ann. *Healing Through Meditation and Prayer.* Virginia Beach, VA: A.R.E. Press, 1978.

Sanford, John A. *Healing and Wholeness.* New York: Paulist Press, 1977.

Shealy, C. Norman, and Caroline M. Myss. *The Creation of Health.* Walpole, NH: Stillpoint, 1988.

Sheikh, Anees A., and Katharina S. Sheikh, eds. *Eastern & Western Approaches to Healing.* New York: John Wiley, 1989.

The Spindrift Papers: Exploring Prayer and Healing Through the Experimental Test. Spindrift, Inc: Lansdale, PA, 1993.

Whitmont, Edward C. *The Alchemy of Healing: Psyche and Soma*. Berkeley: North Atlantic, 1993.

UNEXPECTED OR "MIRACULOUS" HEALING

Guiley, Rosemary Ellen. *The Miracle of Prayer: True Stories of Blessed Healings*. New York: Pocket Books, 1995.

Hirshberg, Caryle, and Marc Ian Barasch. *Remarkable Recovery*. New York: Riverhead, 1995

Lewis, C. S. *Miracles*. New York: Macmillan, 1960.

O'Regan, Brendan, and Caryle Hirshberg. *Spontaneous Remission: An Annotated Bibliography*. Sausalito, CA: Institute of Noetic Sciences, 1993

Rogo, D. Scott. *Miracles*. New York: HarperCollins/Aquarian, 1991.

Siegel, Bernie. *Love, Medicine, and Miracles*. New York: Harper & Row, 1986.

Thurston, Herbert. *The Physical Phenomena of Mysticism*. London: Burns Oates, 1952.

Wakefield, Dan. *Expect a Miracle: The Miraculous Things That Happen to Ordinary People*. New York: HarperCollins, 1995.

Weil, Andrew. *Spontaneous Healing*. New York: Knopf, 1995.

Wilson, Ian. *Stigmata*. San Francisco: Harper & Row, 1989.

THE MIND-BODY CONNECTION AND THE ROLE OF CONSCIOUSNESS IN HEALTH

Achterberg, Jeanne, Larry Dossey, James S. Gordon, et al. *Expanding Medical Horizons*. Section on "Mind-Body Interventions." This

landmark report was commissioned by the Office of Alternative
Medicine of the National Institutes of Health. NIH Publication
No. 94–066. Washington, DC: U. S. Government Printing Office,
1995. (Available from Superintendent of Documents, P.O. Box
371954, Pittsburgh, PA 15250–7954.)

Benson, Herbert, and Eileen M. Stuart. *The Wellness Book*. New York:
Birch Lane Press, 1992.

Borysenko, Joan. *Minding the Body, Mending the Mind*. New York:
Bantam, 1988.

Cousins, Norman. *Head First: The Biology of Hope*. New York: Dutton, 1989.

Dienstfrey, Harris. *Where the Mind Meets the Body*. New York:
HarperCollins, 1991.

Dreher, Henry. *The Immune Power Personality*. New York: Dutton,
1995.

Goleman, Daniel, and Joel Gurin, eds. *Mind-Body Medicine: How to
Use Your Mind for Better Health*. New York: Consumer Reports
Books, 1993.

Justice, Blair. *Who Gets Sick: Thinking and Health*. Houston: Peak
Press, 1987.

Kane, Jeff. *Be Sick Well*. Oakland, CA: New Harbinger, 1991.

Locke, Steven, and Douglas Colligan. *The Healer Within*. New York:
Dutton, 1986.

Northrup, Christiane. *Women's Bodies, Women's Wisdom: Creating
Physical and Emotional Health and Healing*. New York: Bantam,
1994.

Pelletier, Kenneth. *Sound Mind, Sound Body*. New York: Simon &
Schuster, 1994.

Rossi, Ernest L. *The Psychobiology of Mind-Body Healing*. New York: Norton, 1986.

Rossi, Ernest L., and David B. Cheek. *Mind-Body Therapy*. New York: Norton, 1988.

NURSES AND HEALING

Nurses have kept alive the spirit of healing in the West for centuries. There are currently 2.5 million practicing nurses in our country. Here are some of their works that emphasize a body-mind-spirit approach, many of which are written for laypersons as well as for nurses.

Chulay, Marianne, Cathie E. Guzzetta, and Barbara Dossey. *AACN Handbook of Critical Care*. Norwalk, CT: Appleton Lange, forthcoming.

Dossey, Barbara, Lynn Keegan, Cathie E. Guzzetta, and Leslie Kolkmeier. *Holistic Nursing: A Handbook for Practice*. Gaithersburg, MD: Aspen, 1995.

Frisch, Noreen Cavan, and Jane Kelley. *Healing Life's Crises: A Guide for Nurses*. New York: Delmar, 1996.

Hover-Kramer, Dorothea. *Healing Touch: A Resource for Health Care Professionals*. New York: Delmar, 1996.

Keegan, Lynn. *The Nurse As Healer*. New York: Delmar, 1994.

Krieger, Dolores. *Accepting Your Power to Heal*. Santa Fe: Bear, 1993.

Macrae, Janet. *Therapeutic Touch: A Practical Guide*. New York: Knopf, 1991.

Quinn, Janet F. *Therapeutic Touch: A Home Study Video Course for Family Caregivers*. New York: National League for Nursing, 1996. 800–669–9656, ext. 138.

Rew, Lynn. *Awareness in Healing.* New York: Delmar, 1996.

Sayre-Adams, Jean, and Steve Wright. *The Theory and Practice of Therapeutic Touch.* New York: Churchill Livingstone, 1995.

IMAGERY, RITUAL, AND CEREMONY

Achterberg, Jeanne. *Imagery in Healing.* Boston: Shambhala, 1985.

Achterberg, Jeanne, Barbara Dossey, and Leslie Kolkmeier. *Rituals of Healing.* New York: Bantam, 1994.

Brigham, Deirdre Davis. *Imagery for Getting Well.* New York: Norton, 1994.

Cahill, Sedonia, and Joshua Halpern. *Ceremonial Circle.* San Francisco: HarperSanFrancisco, 1992.

Dossey, Barbara M., Lynn Keegan, and Cathie E. Guzzetta. *The Art of Caring.* Four-audiocassette series. Boulder: Sounds True Audio, 1996. 800–333–9185.

Naparstek, Belleruth. *Staying Well with Guided Imagery.* New York: Warner, 1994.

Shames, Karilee Halo. *Creative Imagery in Nursing.* New York: Delmar, 1996.

Simonton, O. Carl, and Reid Henson. *The Healing Journey.* New York: Bantam, 1994.

Simonton, O. Carl, Stephanie Matthews-Simonton, and James L. Creighton. *Getting Well Again.* New York: Bantam, 1992.

PSYCHOLOGICAL AND SPIRITUAL APPROACHES TO HEALING

Achterberg, Jeanne. *Woman as Healer.* Boston: Shambhala, 1990.

Allen, Pat B. *Art Is a Way of Knowing: A Guide to Self-Knowledge and*

Spiritual Fulfillment Through Creativity. Boston: Shambhala, 1995.

Barasch, Marc Ian. *The Healing Path.* New York: Tarcher/Putnam, 1993.

Bloomfield, Harold. *The Power of Five.* New York: Rodale Press, 1994.

Borysenko, Joan. *Fire in the Soul.* New York: Warner, 1993.

Campbell, Don. *Music and Miracles.* Wheaton, IL: Quest, 1992.

——, ed. *Music, Physician for Times to Come.* Wheaton, IL: 1992.

Chopra, Deepak. *Quantum Healing.* New York: Bantam, 1989.

——. *Creating Health.* Boston: Houghton Mifflin, 1987.

Cortis, Bruno. *Heart and Soul.* New York: Villard, 1995.

Curtis, Donald. *Your Thoughts Can Change Your Life.* New York: Warner Books, 1996.

——. *Helping Heaven Happen.* York Beach, Maine: Samuel Weiser, 1992.

——. *Human Problems and How to Solve Them.* North Hollywood, CA: Wilshire Book Co., 1974.

Duff, Kat. *The Alchemy of Illness.* New York: Pantheon, 1993.

Ellsworth, Robert, and Janet Ellsworth. *How Shall We Love?* New York: Putnam, 1996.

Evans, Donald. *Spiritualty and Human Nature.* Albany: SUNY Press, 1993.

Frank, Arthur W. *The Wounded Storyteller: Body, Illness, and Ethics.* Chicago: University of Chicago Press, 1995.

——. *At the Will of the Body: Reflections on Illness.* Boston: Houghton Mifflin, 1991.

Gordon, James S. *Manifesto for a New Medicine: Your Guide to Healing.* Reading, MA: Addison-Wesley, 1996.

Grasse, Ray. *The Waking Dream.* Wheaton, IL: Quest, 1996.

Hendricks, Gay, and Kathleen Hendricks. *At the Speed of Life*. New York: Bantam, 1993.

Huang, Chungliang Al, and Jerry Lynch. *Thinking Body, Dancing Mind*. New York: Bantam, 1992.

Ingerman, Sandra. *Welcome Home: Life After Healing*. San Francisco: HarperSanFrancisco, 1993.

Jensen, Lone. *Gifts of Grace*. New York: HarperCollins, 1995.

Jones, James W. *In the Middle of This Road We Call Life*. San Francisco: HarperSanFrancisco, 1994.

Justice, Rita. *Alive and Well*. Houston: Peak Press, 1995.

Kabat-Zinn, Jon. *Wherever You Go, There You Are*. New York: Hyperion, 1994.

Lawlis, G. Frank. *Transpersonal Medicine*. Boston: Shambhala, 1996.

LeShan, Lawrence. *Cancer as a Turning Point*. New York: Dutton, 1989.

Linthorst, Ann. *Soul-Kissed*. New York: Crossroad Publishing, 1995.

Luce, Gay Gaer. *Longer Life, More Joy*. North Hollywood, CA: Newcastle, 1992.

Miller, Timothy. *How to Want What You Have*. New York: Henry Holt, 1995.

Moss, Richard. *The Second Miracle*. Berkeley: Celestial Arts, 1995.

Muller, Wayne. *How, Then, Shall We Live?* New York: Bantam, 1995.

Myss, Caroline. *Anatomy of the Spirit*. New York: Harmony, 1996.

Nachman, Rabbi. *Outpouring of the Soul*. Jerusalem: Reslov Research Institute, 1980.

Pearsall, Paul. *Making Miracles*. New York: Prentice-Hall, 1991.

Remen, Rachel Naomi. *Wounded Healers*. Mill Valley, CA: Wounded Healer Press, 1995.

Sardello, Robert. *Love and the Soul.* New York: HarperCollins, 1995.

Small, Jacquelyn. *Embodying Spirit.* New York: HarperCollins, 1994.

———. *Awakening in Time.* New York: Bantam, 1991.

Vaughan, Frances. *The Inward Arc: Healing in Psychotherapy and Spirituality.* Grass Valley, CA: Blue Dolphin, 1995.

———. *Shadows of the Sacred.* Wheaton, IL: Quest, 1995.

Wilber, Ken. *Sex, Ecology, Spirituality.* Boston: Shambhala, 1995.

SHAMANIC AND NATIVE HEALING

Blum, Ralph H. *The Book of Runes.* New York: St. Martin's, 1982.

Blum, Ralph H., and Susan Loughan. *The Healing Runes.* New York: St. Martin's, 1995.

Cohen, Kenneth S. *Strong As the Mountain, Supple As Water: The Way of Qigong.* New York: Ballantine, 1996.

Ingerman, Sandra. *Soul Retrieval: Mending the Fragmented Self.* San Francisco: HarperSanFrancisco, 1991.

Kalweit, Holger. *Shamans, Healers and Medicine Men.* Boston: Shambhala, 1992.

Krippner, Stanley, and Alberto Villoldo. *The Realms of Healing.* Berkeley: Celestial Arts, 1976.

Krippner, Stanley, and Patrick Welch. *Spiritual Dimensions of Healing.* New York: Irvington, 1992.

Lawlis, G. Frank. *The Cure: The Hero's Journey with Cancer,* and *The Caregiver's Guide to the Cure.* San Jose: Resource Publications, 1994

Rinpoche, Sogyal. *The Tibetan Book of Living and Dying.* San Francisco: HarperSanFrancisco, 1992.

Sams, Jamie. *Earth Medicine.* San Francisco: HarperSanFrancisco, 1994.

———. *The Sacred Path Cards* and *The Sacred Path Workbook.* San Francisco: HarperSanFrancisco, 1990 and 1991, resp.

Sams, Jamie, and David Carson. *The Medicine Cards.* Santa Fe: Bear, 1988.

Villoldo, Alberto, and Stanley Krippner. *Healing States.* New York: Simon & Schuster/Fireside, 1987.

Wesselman, Hank. *Spiritwalker.* New York: Bantam, 1995.

SCIENCE, CONSCIOUSNESS, AND SPIRIT

Abraham, Ralph, Terence McKenna, and Rupert Sheldrake. *Trialogues at the Edge of the West.* Santa Fe: Bear, 1992.

Bohm, David. *Wholeness and the Implicate Order.* Boston: Routledge and Kegan Paul, 1980.

Davies, Paul. *God and the New Physics.* New York: Simon & Schuster, 1983.

Friedman, Norman. *Bridging Science and Spirit.* St. Louis: Living Lake Books, 1990.

Goswami, Amit, with Richard E. Reed and Maggie Goswami. *The Self-Aware Universe.* New York: Putnam, 1993.

Herbert, Nick. *Elemental Mind.* New York: Dutton, 1993.

———. *Quantum Reality.* New York: Anchor/Doubleday, 1987.

Jahn, Robert G., ed. *The Role of Consciousness in the Physical World.* AAAS Selected Symposium. Boulder, CO: Westview, 1981.

Jahn, Robert G., and Brenda J. Dunne. *Margins of Reality: The Role of Consciousness in the Physical World.* New York: Harcourt Brace Jovanovich, 1987.

Josephson, B. D., and V. S. Ramachandran, eds. *Consciousness and the Physical World*. New York: Pergamon, 1980.

Pearce, Joseph Chilton. *Evolution's End*. San Francisco: HarperSan-Francisco,1992.

Polkinghorne, John. *Science and Creation: The Search for Understanding*. Boston: Shambhala, 1989.

———. *Science and Providence: God's Interaction with the World*. Boston: Shambhala, 1989.

Ravindra, Ravi, ed. *Science and Spirit*. New York: Paragon, 1991.

Sheldrake, Rupert. *Seven Experiments that Could Change the World*. New York: Riverhead, 1995.

Thompson, Richard L. *Mechanistic and Nonmechanistic Science*. Los Angeles: Bhaktivedanta Book Trust, 1981.

Wolf, Fred Alan. *Taking the Quantum Leap*. New York: Harper & Row, 1981.

GUILT AND ILLNESS

Borysenko, Joan. *Guilt Is the Teacher, Love Is the Lesson*. New York: Warner, 1990

Kavanaugh, James. *God Lives: From Religious Guilt to Spiritual Freedom*. Highland Park, IL: Steven J. Nash, 1993.

Wilber, Ken. *Grace and Grit*. Boston: Shambhala: 1991.

Grateful acknowledgment is made to the following for permission to quote from their work:

To Rudolph Barden, Dorothy Martin, and Stephanie R. Waugh for excerpts from personal correspondence.

To Deborah Rose, former vice president of Spindrift, Inc., for various excerpts from *Home Catacomb*, September 1994 and November 1995; and to Betsy MacGregor, M.D., and *Advances* magazine for excerpts from "Health Reform and the Sacred," Advances 11, no. 1 (Winter 1995).

AUTHOR'S REQUEST

My research in prayer continues. I would appreciate hearing from readers who would be willing to share their experiences. I am especially interested in "hopeless" situations in which ordinary medical interventions failed but in which prayer seemed to work. In addition, I am exploring four additional areas discussed in my book *Healing Words*: negative prayer effects, prayers involving dreams, time-displaced prayer, and telesomatic events. Please write to me at the following address:

Larry Dossey, M.D.
223 N. Guadalupe, #169
Santa Fe, NM 87501

Thank you.